# MICHAEL GATHIMA

# computer programming for toddlers teacher edition

*comprehensive python programing for toddlers*

# Contents

# 1

# Preface

Welcome to "Comprehensive Computer Programming for Toddlers: Teacher's Guide"!

Teaching young children how to program is an exciting and rewarding journey. This guide was born from my personal experience teaching my daughter, Cleopatra, who was 7 at the time and is now 9. Despite the challenges, the joy of seeing her understand and create with code inspired me to create a resource that could help other parents and teachers.

In today's digital world, understanding programming from a young age offers numerous benefits. It enhances problem-solving skills, fosters creativity, and builds confidence. By learning to code, children gain a solid foundation in logical thinking that will serve them in any future endeavor.

This teacher's guide is designed to complement the "Comprehensive Computer Programming for Toddlers" student book. It provides detailed explanations, fun activities, and teaching strategies to make the learning experience engaging and effective. You will find tips on how to break down complex topics into simple concepts, assess progress, and keep young learners motivated.

Let's embark on this adventure together and unlock the potential of every young coder!

# 2

# Level 1 Beginner

## Introduction to Python

- **Python installation and setup**

Installing Python and Setting up the Environment **Objective: Help young children install Python in an engaging and interactive way.**

1. **Introduction:**
2. Explain to the children that Python is a tool they will use to create fun projects. Compare Python to a magic wand that needs to be set up before it can create magic.
3. **Downloading Python:**
4. Guide the children to the python.org website. Use engaging language, like introducing "Pip the Python" who needs a home.
5. **Example:** "Let's go to Pip's website and download his special house."

6. **Installation Process:**
7. Walk the children through the installation process step-by-step. Ensure they understand each step by using simple and relatable terms.
8. **Example:** "Click on the button that says 'Install Now' to build Pip's house."
9. **Visual and Interactive Elements:**
10. Use pictures or videos to show each step of the installation. You can create a fun character, like Pip the Python, to make the process more engaging.
11. **Checking Installation:**
12. Teach the children how to check if Python is installed correctly by using the Command Prompt.
13. **Example:** "We need to ask Pip if he's ready by typing a secret code: python —version."
14. **Reinforcement:**
15. Celebrate the completion of the installation with a fun activity or a reward. This will create a positive association with the learning process.
16. **Example:** "Great job! Pip is ready to help us create magic. Let's draw a picture of Pip's new home."

# 3

# IDEs (Integrated Development Environments)

Using IDEs: Introducing Thonny to Young Children

bjective: Introduce young children to IDEs and guide them through using Thonny for the first time.

1. **Introduction to IDEs:**

- Explain that an IDE is a special environment where they can write and test their Python code. Compare it to a playground where they can safely explore and create.
- **Example:** "An IDE is like a magic drawing board where we can create our Python stories."

1. **Choosing Thonny:**

- Thonny is an ideal choice for beginners due to its simplicity and ease of use. It provides a straightforward interface that helps children focus on coding without being overwhelmed.

1. **Downloading Thonny:**

- Guide the children to thonny.org and help them download the appropriate version for their computer.
- **Example:** "Let's visit Thonny's website and download our magic drawing board."

1. **Installation Process:**

- Walk the children through the installation steps. Use simple and engaging language to explain each step.
- **Example:** "Click on 'Next' a few times, then 'Install,' and finally 'Finish' to set up Thonny."

1. **First Steps in Thonny:**

- Show the children how to open Thonny and explain the main parts of the interface (editor area, console, etc.).
- **Example:** "This big white area is where we will write our Python magic, and the bottom part will show us the results."

1. **Writing and Running the First Program:**

- Guide the children to write their first simple program. Use a familiar and fun example.

- **Example:** "Let's type print("Hello, world!") in the big white area and press the green play button to see the magic happen."

1. **Interactive Exploration:**

- Encourage the children to explore and try different simple commands. Offer support and celebrate their successes.
- **Example:** "Try typing print("Your Name") and see what happens!"

1. **Reinforcement:**

- Reinforce the learning experience with a small reward or a fun activity. This positive reinforcement will help build their confidence and interest.
- **Example:** "Great job! Let's draw a picture of what we coded today."

- Writing and running your first Python program

# 4

# Python syntax and semantics

F or Teachers:

Teaching Python Syntax and Semantics

**Objective: Help young children understand the basic syntax and semantics of Python through engaging examples and activities.**

1. **Introduction to Syntax and Semantics:**

- Explain that syntax is like the grammar of Python and semantics is the meaning behind the code. Use simple analogies to make it relatable.
- **Example:** "Syntax is like the rules we follow to make sentences, and semantics is the story our sentences tell."

1. **Writing Basic Syntax:**

- Start with the print function to show how to display messages.
- **Example:** "The print function is like a magic spell that makes Python show messages on the screen."

1. **Explaining Semantics:**

- Describe how the meaning of code is conveyed through correct syntax.
- **Example:** "When we write print("Hello, world!"), it means we want Python to show the message 'Hello, world!' on the screen."

1. **Hands-On Practice:**

- Encourage the children to write their own print statements with different messages.
- **Example:** "Type print("I love coding!") and press the play button. What do you see?"

1. **Introducing Special Characters:**

- Explain the use of special characters like # for comments and : for colons.
- **Example:** "The # symbol is used to write notes that Python will ignore. Try writing # This is a note in your code."

1. **Handling Errors:**

- Teach children that making mistakes is part of learning.

Show how to read error messages and correct syntax mistakes.

- **Example:** "If we make a mistake, Python will tell us what went wrong. Let's fix it together and try again."

1. **Reinforcement:**

- Use interactive activities and rewards to reinforce learning.
- **Example:** "Great job! Let's draw a picture of what our code did today."

1. **Storytelling with Code:**

- Encourage creativity by letting children write short stories with code.
- **Example:** "Write a story using print that tells something fun about your day."

# 5

# Basic Data Types(chapter2)

Numbers (integers, floats)

Teaching Basic Data Types: Numbers (Integers
and Floats)
   Objective: Help young children understand and
work with integers and floats in Python through simple
and engaging activities.

1. **Introduction to Integers and Floats:**

- Explain that integers are whole numbers, and floats are
  numbers with decimal points. Use everyday examples to
  make it relatable.
- **Example:** "Integers are like the number of apples you
  have, and floats are like the price of an apple in dollars and
  cents."

1. **Using Thonny to Demonstrate:**

- Show how to print integers and floats using simple examples in Thonny.
- **Example:** "Let's type print(5) for an integer and print(3.14) for a float."

1. **Hands-On Practice:**

- Encourage the children to type different integers and floats and see the output.
- **Example:** "Try typing print(-10) and print(2.5) to see negative integers and floats."

1. **Arithmetic Operations:**

- Teach basic arithmetic operations (addition, subtraction, multiplication, and division) using integers and floats.
- **Example:** "Let's add 5 + 3 and see what Python shows us."

1. **Mixing Integers and Floats:**

- Show examples of mixing integers and floats in arithmetic operations.
- **Example:** "What happens if we add an integer and a float, like 5 + 2.5?"

1. **Interactive Exploration:**

- Provide simple math problems for the children to solve using Python.
- **Example:** "Type print(7 * 1.5) and see what the answer is."

1. **Visual Aids:**

- Use visual aids such as number lines or drawings to illustrate the difference between integers and floats.
- **Example:** "Draw a number line showing whole numbers (integers) and points in between (floats)."

1. **Reinforcement:**

- Reinforce learning with fun activities, such as drawing or storytelling using numbers.
- **Example:** "Let's draw a picture of how many apples we have and their prices using integers and floats."

## Strings

### Teaching Strings in Python
**Objective: Help young children understand and work with strings in Python through engaging examples and activities.**

1. **Introduction to Strings:**

- Explain that strings are sequences of characters enclosed in quotes. Use simple examples to illustrate.
- **Example:** "Strings are like words or sentences we write inside quotes. They help us talk to the computer."

1. **Writing Strings:**

13

- Show how to write strings using single, double, and triple quotes.
- **Example:** "Let's write print("Hello, world!") and see what happens."

1. **Combining Strings:**

- Teach how to concatenate strings using the + symbol.
- **Example:** "We can join strings together with the + symbol. Try print("Hello, " + "world!")."

1. **Repeating Strings:**

- Demonstrate repeating strings using the * symbol.
- **Example:** "Let's repeat a string using print("Hello! " * 3)."

1. **Hands-On Practice:**

- Encourage the children to write their own strings and experiment with combining and repeating them.
- **Example:** "Type print("I love coding! " * 2) and see the result."

1. **Interactive Exploration:**

- Provide simple tasks for the children to practice strings.
- **Example:** "Create a string with your name and print it. Then, combine it with another string."

1. **Visual Aids:**

- Use visual aids to show how strings are formed and manipulated.
- **Example:** "Draw a picture of a string as a chain of characters inside quotes."

1. **Reinforcement:**

- Reinforce learning with fun activities, like creating short stories or messages using strings.
- **Example:** "Write a short story using strings and print it in Python."

# Booleans

**Teaching Booleans in Python**
   **Objective: Help young children understand and work with Booleans in Python through engaging examples and activities.**

1. **Introduction to Booleans:**

- Explain that Booleans are a data type with only two possible values: True and False. Use simple analogies to make it relatable.
- **Example:** "Booleans are like a light switch. It can be either on (True) or off (False)."

1. **Writing Booleans:**

- Show how to write Booleans using True and False with capital T and F.
- **Example:** "Let's type print(True) and print(False) and see what happens."

1. **Using Booleans in Comparisons:**

- Teach how to use Booleans with comparison operators (>, <, ==, !=, >=, <=).
- **Example:** "We can compare numbers to see if something is true or false. Try print(5 > 3)."

1. **Hands-On Practice:**

- Encourage the children to write their own comparisons and see the output.
- **Example:** "Type print(10 == 10) and see what Python says."

1. **Interactive Exploration:**

- Provide simple tasks for the children to practice using Booleans.
- **Example:** "Create comparisons with your favorite numbers and check if they are true or false."

1. **Visual Aids:**

- Use visual aids to illustrate how comparisons work and the concept of true and false.
- **Example:** "Draw pictures showing different comparisons,

like 5 > 3 and 2 < 1."

1. **Reinforcement:**

- Reinforce learning with fun activities, like making decisions based on true or false conditions.
- **Example:** "Write a short program that makes decisions based on comparisons, like checking if a number is greater than another."

1. **Variables and Constants**

## Variable naming conventions

**Teaching Variable Naming Conventions**
  **Objective:** **Help young children understand how to name variables in Python through engaging examples and activities.**

1. **Introduction to Variables:**

- Explain that variables are like containers (or magic boxes) where we store values. Use simple analogies to make it relatable.
- **Example:** "Variables are like boxes with names where we can keep our toys (values)."

1. **Naming Conventions:**

17

- Teach the rules for naming variables:

1. Start with a letter or an underscore.
2. Use letters, numbers, and underscores, but no spaces.
3. Use lowercase letters for simple names.

- **Example:** "Let's name our box my_number and put a number inside it."

1. **Good and Bad Examples:**

- Show examples of good and bad variable names and explain why.
- **Example:** "We can name a box total_score, but not 1score."

1. **Hands-On Practice:**

- Encourage the children to name their own variables and store values in them.
- **Example:** "Type age = 10 and see what happens when you print age."

1. **Interactive Exploration:**

- Provide simple tasks for the children to practice naming variables.
- **Example:** "Create a variable for your favorite color and print it."

1. **Visual Aids:**

- Use visual aids to show how variables are named and used.
- **Example:** "Draw a picture of a box named my_number and put a number inside it."

1. **Reinforcement:**

- Reinforce learning with fun activities, like creating stories with named variables.
- **Example:** "Write a short story using variables like name, age, and favorite_toy."

# Constants

**Teaching Constants in Python**

Objective: Help young children understand the concept of constants in Python through engaging examples and activities.

1. **Introduction to Constants:**

- Explain that constants are special variables whose values do not change. Use simple analogies to make it relatable.
- **Example:** "Constants are like labels for things that never change, like the number of days in a week."

1. **Naming Conventions:**

- Teach that constants are usually written in all capital letters with underscores separating words.

- **Example:** "We name constants with all capital letters, like PI and GRAVITY."

1. **Examples of Constants:**

- Provide examples of constants and their usage.
- **Example:** "Type PI = 3.14 and print(PI) to see the constant for pi."

1. **Hands-On Practice:**

- Encourage the children to create their own constants and use them in simple programs.
- **Example:** "Create a constant for the speed of light with SPEED_OF_LIGHT = 299792458."

1. **Interactive Exploration:**

- Provide tasks for the children to practice using constants.
- **Example:** "Create constants for your favorite numbers and print them."

1. **Visual Aids:**

- Use visual aids to illustrate how constants are named and used.
- **Example:** "Draw a picture of a box named GRAVITY and put the number 9.8 inside it."

1. **Reinforcement:**

- Reinforce learning with fun activities, like creating a list of important constants and their values.
- **Example:** "Write a short story using constants like PI, GRAVITY, and SPEED_OF_LIGHT."

# 6

# Basic Operators(chapter 3)

Arithmetic operators

Teaching Arithmetic Operators
Objective: Help young children understand and use arithmetic operators in Python through engaging examples and activities.

1. **Introduction to Arithmetic Operators:**

- Explain that arithmetic operators are symbols that help us perform basic math operations.
- **Example:** "Arithmetic operators like +, -, *, and / help us add, subtract, multiply, and divide numbers."

1. **Addition (+):**

- Show how to use the + operator to add two numbers.
- **Example:** "Type print(5 + 3) to see the result of adding 5 and 3."

1. **Subtraction (-):**

- Show how to use the - operator to subtract one number from another.
- **Example:** "Type print(9 - 4) to see the result of subtracting 4 from 9."

1. **Multiplication (*):**

- Show how to use the * operator to multiply two numbers.
- **Example:** "Type print(7 * 2) to see the result of multiplying 7 and 2."

1. **Division (/):**

- Show how to use the / operator to divide one number by another.
- **Example:** "Type print(10 / 2) to see the result of dividing 10 by 2."

1. **Hands-On Practice:**

- Encourage the children to write their own math problems and solve them with Python.
- **Example:** "Type print(15 + 5) and see the result."

1. **Interactive Exploration:**

23

- Provide simple tasks for the children to practice using arithmetic operators.
- **Example:** "Create your own math problems and solve them using +, -, *, and /."

1. **Visual Aids:**

- Use visual aids to show how arithmetic operations work.
- **Example:** "Draw pictures of addition, subtraction, multiplication, and division problems."

1. **Reinforcement:**

- Reinforce learning with fun activities, like solving math puzzles using Python.
- **Example:** "Write a short program to solve a series of math problems."

# Comparison operators

**Teaching Comparison Operators**
   **Objective:** **Help young children understand and use comparison operators in Python through engaging examples and activities.**

1. **Introduction to Comparison Operators:**

- Explain that comparison operators are symbols that help us compare two values and decide if they are true or false.

- **Example:** "Comparison operators like >, <, ==, !=, >=, and <= help us see if numbers are bigger, smaller, equal, or different."

1. **Greater Than (>):**

- Show how to use the > operator to check if one number is bigger than another.
- **Example:** "Type print(5 > 3) to see if 5 is greater than 3."

1. **Less Than (<):**

- Show how to use the < operator to check if one number is smaller than another.
- **Example:** "Type print(2 < 4) to see if 2 is less than 4."

1. **Equal To (==):**

- Show how to use the == operator to check if two numbers are the same.
- **Example:** "Type print(7 == 7) to see if 7 is equal to 7."

1. **Not Equal To (!=):**

- Show how to use the != operator to check if two numbers are different.
- **Example:** "Type print(5 != 3) to see if 5 is not equal to 3."

1. **Greater Than or Equal To (>=):**

- Show how to use the >= operator to check if one number

is bigger than or the same as another.
- **Example:** "Type print(6 >= 6) to see if 6 is greater than or equal to 6."

1. **Less Than or Equal To (<=):**

- Show how to use the <= operator to check if one number is smaller than or the same as another.
- **Example:** "Type print(3 <= 5) to see if 3 is less than or equal to 5."

1. **Hands-On Practice:**

- Encourage the children to write their own comparisons and see the output.
- **Example:** "Type print(10 > 8) and see if 10 is greater than 8."

1. **Interactive Exploration:**

- Provide simple tasks for the children to practice using comparison operators.
- **Example:** "Create comparisons with your favorite numbers and check if they are true or false."

1. **Visual Aids:**

- Use visual aids to show how comparison operations work.
- **Example:** "Draw pictures showing different comparisons, like 5 > 3 and 2 < 4."

1. **Reinforcement:**

- Reinforce learning with fun activities, like making decisions based on true or false conditions.
- **Example:** "Write a short program that makes decisions based on comparisons, like checking if a number is greater than another."

## Logical operators

**Teaching Logical Operators**
**Objective: Help young children understand and use logical operators in Python through engaging examples and activities.**

1. **Introduction to Logical Operators:**

- Explain that logical operators are special words that help us combine multiple true or false statements.
- **Example:** "Logical operators like and, or, and not help us make decisions based on multiple conditions."

1. **AND (and):**

- Show how to use the and operator to check if both conditions are true.
- **Example:** "Type print(True and True) to see if both conditions are true."

1. **OR (or):**

- Show how to use the or operator to check if at least one condition is true.
- **Example:** "Type print(True or False) to see if at least one condition is true."

1. **NOT (not):**

- Show how to use the not operator to flip the true or false value.
- **Example:** "Type print(not True) to see the opposite of true."

1. **Hands-On Practice:**

- Encourage the children to write their own true or false statements and see the results.
- **Example:** "Type print(5 > 3 and 2 < 4) to see if both conditions are true."

1. **Interactive Exploration:**

- Provide simple tasks for the children to practice using logical operators.
- **Example:** "Create statements with and, or, and not and check if they are true or false."

1. **Visual Aids:**

- Use visual aids to show how logical operations work.

- **Example:** "Draw pictures showing different logical statements, like True and False and not True."

1. **Reinforcement:**

- Reinforce learning with fun activities, like making decisions based on true or false conditions.
- **Example:** "Write a short program that makes decisions based on logical operators, like checking if multiple conditions are true."

## Assignment operators

**Teaching Assignment Operators**
   **Objective:** Help young children understand and use assignment operators in Python through engaging examples and activities.

1. **Introduction to Assignment Operators:**

- Explain that assignment operators are symbols that help us assign values to variables and modify them.
- **Example:** "Assignment operators like =, +=, -=, *=, and /= help us give values to variables and change them."

1. **The Basic Assignment (=):**

- Show how to use the = operator to assign a value to a variable.

29

- **Example:** "Type toy = 'car' to assign the value 'car' to the variable toy."

1. **Add and Assign (+=):**

- Show how to use the += operator to add a value to the variable's current value.
- **Example:** "Type score += 5 to add 5 to the current value of score."

1. **Subtract and Assign (-=):**

- Show how to use the -= operator to subtract a value from the variable's current value.
- **Example:** "Type score -= 3 to subtract 3 from the current value of score."

1. **Multiply and Assign (\*=):**

- Show how to use the \*= operator to multiply the variable's value by another value.
- **Example:** "Type stars \*= 2 to double the current value of stars."

1. **Divide and Assign (/=):**

- Show how to use the /= operator to divide the variable's value by another value.
- **Example:** "Type apples /= 2 to divide the current value of apples by 2."

1. **Hands-On Practice:**

- Encourage the children to write their own examples using assignment operators and see the results.
- **Example:** "Type candies = 20, then candies -= 4 and candies += 10 to see how many candies we have now."

1. **Interactive Exploration:**

- Provide simple tasks for the children to practice using assignment operators.
- **Example:** "Create variables for balloons, cookies, and candies, and use assignment operators to change their values."

1. **Visual Aids:**

- Use visual aids to show how assignment operators work.
- **Example:** "Draw pictures showing different assignment operations, like adding and subtracting values from variables."

1. **Reinforcement:**

- Reinforce learning with fun activities, like making stories where they use assignment operators to change values.
- **Example:** "Write a short story where you have to add, subtract, multiply, or divide values using assignment operators."

# Chapter 4 Control Flow

## Conditional statements (if, elif, else)

Teaching Conditional Statements: If, Elif, and Else Objective: Help young children understand and use conditional statements in Python through engaging examples and activities.

1. **Introduction to Conditional Statements:**

- Explain that conditional statements help us make decisions in our programs.
- **Example:** "Conditional statements like if, elif, and else help us choose what to do based on different conditions."

1. **Using "If" Statements:**

- Show how to use the if statement to check if a condition is true.

- **Example:** "Type if weather == 'sunny': to check if the weather is sunny."

1. **Using "Elif" Statements:**

- Show how to use the elif statement to check another condition if the first one isn't true.
- **Example:** "Type elif weather == 'rainy': to check if the weather is rainy."

1. **Using "Else" Statements:**

- Show how to use the else statement to do something if none of the previous conditions are true.
- **Example:** "Type else: to do something if the weather is neither sunny nor rainy."

1. **Hands-On Practice:**

- Encourage the children to write their own examples using conditional statements and see the results.
- **Example:** "Type favorite_toy = 'doll', then use if, elif, and else to decide what to play with based on the toy."

1. **Interactive Exploration:**

- Provide simple tasks for the children to practice using conditional statements.
- **Example:** "Create a game where they decide what to do based on the weather or their favorite toy."

1. **Visual Aids:**

- Use visual aids to show how conditional statements work.
- **Example:** "Draw pictures showing different conditions, like sunny, rainy, and cold weather, and what actions to take for each."

1. **Reinforcement:**

- Reinforce learning with fun activities, like making stories where they use conditional statements to make decisions.
- **Example:** "Write a short story where they decide what to do based on different conditions using if, elif, and else."

# 8

# chapter 5 Loops (for, while)

Teaching Loops: For and While
Objective: Help young children understand and use loops in Python through engaging examples and activities.

1. **Introduction to Loops:**

- Explain that loops help us repeat actions in our programs.
- **Example:** "Loops like for and while help us do things over and over again without having to write the same code multiple times."

1. **Using "For" Loops:**

- Show how to use the for loop to repeat actions a certain number of times.
- **Example:** "Type for i in range(1, 6): to repeat an action five times."

1. **Using "While" Loops:**

- Show how to use the while loop to repeat actions as long as a condition is true.
- **Example:** "Type while not tired: to keep repeating an action until we get tired."

1. **Hands-On Practice:**

- Encourage the children to write their own examples using loops and see the results.
- **Example:** "Type for i in range(5): print('I love my doll') to repeat a message five times."

1. **Interactive Exploration:**

- Provide simple tasks for the children to practice using loops.
- **Example:** "Create a game where they print their favorite toy multiple times using a for loop and repeat actions until a condition is met using a while loop."

1. **Visual Aids:**

- Use visual aids to show how loops work.
- **Example:** "Draw pictures showing the repeated actions in a loop, like counting from 1 to 5 or singing verses of a song."

1. **Reinforcement:**

- Reinforce learning with fun activities, like making stories where they use loops to repeat actions.
- **Example:** "Write a short story where they use loops to repeat fun activities, like singing a song or playing a game."

## Break and continue statements

**Teaching Break and Continue Statements**

**Objective: Help young children understand and use "break" and "continue" statements in Python through engaging examples and activities.**

1. **Introduction to Break and Continue:**

- Explain that "break" and "continue" help control the flow of loops.
- **Example:** "The break statement stops a loop early, and the continue statement skips to the next iteration of the loop."

1. **Using "Break" Statements:**

- Show how to use the break statement to stop a loop.
- **Example:** "Type if i == 3: break to stop the loop when the number 3 is reached."

1. **Using "Continue" Statements:**

- Show how to use the continue statement to skip an iteration of the loop.
- **Example:** "Type if i == 2: continue to skip the number 2 and continue the loop."

1. **Hands-On Practice:**

- Encourage the children to write their own examples using "break" and "continue" statements.
- **Example:** "Type for i in range(1, 6): if i == 3: break to stop counting when they reach the number 3."

1. **Interactive Exploration:**

- Provide simple tasks for the children to practice using "break" and "continue" statements.
- **Example:** "Create a game where they stop counting when they reach their favorite number using break and skip a number they don't like using continue."

1. **Visual Aids:**

- Use visual aids to show how "break" and "continue" work in loops.
- **Example:** "Draw pictures showing a loop stopping at a certain point for break and skipping an iteration for continue."

1. **Reinforcement:**

38

- Reinforce learning with fun activities, like making stories where they use "break" and "continue" to control actions.
- **Example:** "Write a short story where they use break to stop an action early and continue to skip an action."

# 9

# Chapter 6 Functions

Defining and calling functions

**T**eaching Functions: Defining and Calling Functions
Objective: Help young children understand and use functions in Python through engaging examples and activities.

1. **Introduction to Functions:**

- Explain that functions are sets of instructions that perform a specific task.
- **Example:** "Functions are like magic spells. When you use a spell, it does something special!"

1. **Defining a Function:**

- Show how to define a function using the def keyword, a

name, and a colon.

- **Example:** "Type def say_hello(): to create a function called say_hello."

1. **Calling a Function:**

- Show how to call a function by writing its name followed by parentheses.
- **Example:** "Type say_hello() to call the say_hello function."

1. **Hands-On Practice:**

- Encourage the children to write their own functions and call them.
- **Example:** "Type def animal_sound(): print('Woof! Woof!') to create an animal_sound function and call it with animal_sound()."

1. **Interactive Exploration:**

- Provide simple tasks for the children to practice defining and calling functions.
- **Example:** "Create a function that says their favorite food, like def favorite_food(): print('I love pizza!')."

1. **Visual Aids:**

- Use visual aids to show how functions work.
- **Example:** "Draw a picture of a magic spell book to represent defining functions and a magic wand to represent calling functions."

1. **Reinforcement:**

- Reinforce learning with fun activities, like making stories where they use functions as magic spells to perform actions.
- **Example:** "Write a short story where they create and use magic spells (functions) to make things happen."

## Function arguments and return values

**Teaching Function Arguments and Return Values**
    **Objective: Help young children understand and use function arguments and return values in Python through engaging examples and activities.**

1. **Introduction to Function Arguments:**

- Explain that arguments are inputs given to functions to make them work with specific data.
- **Example:** "Arguments are like special ingredients we add to our functions to make them work better. For instance, greet(name) takes a name as an argument."

1. **Giving Arguments to a Function:**

- Show how to define a function with arguments.
- **Example:** "Type def greet(name): to create a function that takes a name as an argument."

1. **Calling a Function with Arguments:**

- Show how to call a function with specific arguments.
- **Example:** "Type greet("Alice") to call the greet function and give it the name 'Alice.'"

1. **Introduction to Return Values:**

- Explain that return values are the results given back by functions.
- **Example:** "Return values are like the magic results our functions give back to us. For instance, add_numbers(a, b) returns the sum of a and b."

1. **Creating a Function with a Return Value:**

- Show how to define a function that returns a value.
- **Example:** "Type def add_numbers(a, b): return a + b to create a function that adds two numbers and returns the result."

1. **Hands-On Practice:**

- Encourage the children to write their own functions with arguments and return values.
- **Example:** "Type def total_candies(candies1, candies2): return candies1 + candies2 to create a function that calculates the total number of candies."

1. **Interactive Exploration:**

- Provide simple tasks for the children to practice using arguments and return values.
- **Example:** "Create a function that finds the total number of candies and call it with different numbers of candies."

1. **Visual Aids:**

- Use visual aids to show how arguments and return values work.
- **Example:** "Draw pictures showing how functions take in arguments (like ingredients) and give back return values (like magic results)."

1. **Reinforcement:**

- Reinforce learning with fun activities, like making stories where they use arguments and return values to solve problems.
- **Example:** "Write a short story where they create functions that take arguments and return magic results to help solve problems."

# Variable scope

**Teaching Variable Scope**
  **Objective: Help young children understand and use the concept of variable scope in Python through engaging examples and activities.**

1. **Introduction to Variable Scope:**

- Explain that variable scope defines where a variable can be used in the code.
- **Example:** "Variable scope is like a playground. Some toys (variables) can be played with anywhere, while others can only be played with in certain rooms."

1. **Global Scope:**

- Show how variables created outside any function can be used anywhere in the code.
- **Example:** "Type toy = "Magic Ball" outside any function to create a global variable that can be used anywhere."

1. **Local Scope:**

- Show how variables created inside a function can only be used inside that function.
- **Example:** "Type toy = "Magic Car" inside a function to create a local variable that can only be used in that function."

1. **Hands-On Practice:**

- Encourage the children to write their own examples using global and local scope.
- **Example:** "Type def play_with_toy(): toy = "Magic Car" to create a local variable inside a function and toy = "Magic Ball" outside any function for a global variable."

1. **Interactive Exploration:**

- Provide simple tasks for the children to practice using variable scope.
- **Example:** "Create a game where they have different toys for different rooms and see where they can play with each toy."

1. **Visual Aids:**

- Use visual aids to show how global and local scope work.
- **Example:** "Draw pictures of a house with different rooms to represent functions and toys that can be played with everywhere (global scope) or only in certain rooms (local scope)."

1. **Reinforcement:**

- Reinforce learning with fun activities, like making stories where they use variables in different scopes to solve problems.
- **Example:** "Write a short story where they create and use variables in global and local scope to help solve problems in different rooms of a house."

## Lambda functions

**Teaching Lambda Functions**

**Objective:** **Help young children understand and use lambda functions in Python through engaging examples and activities.**

1. **Introduction to Lambda Functions:**

- Explain that lambda functions are small functions that can be created quickly and used for simple tasks.
- **Example:** "Lambda functions are like tiny, magic spells that can do something special quickly without needing a lot of words."

1. **Creating a Lambda Function:**

- Show how to create a lambda function using the lambda keyword.
- **Example:** "Type add = lambda a, b: a + b to create a lambda function that adds two numbers."

1. **Calling a Lambda Function:**

- Show how to use a lambda function by calling it with arguments.
- **Example:** "Type result = add(5, 3) to call the lambda function and get the result."

1. **Hands-On Practice:**

- Encourage the children to create their own lambda functions for simple tasks.
- **Example:** "Type square = lambda x: x * x to create a lambda function that squares a number."

1. **Interactive Exploration:**

- Provide simple tasks for the children to practice using lambda functions.
- **Example:** "Create a lambda function that checks if a number is bigger than 10 and use it to check different numbers."

1. **Visual Aids:**

- Use visual aids to show how lambda functions work.
- **Example:** "Draw a picture of a tiny magic spell that quickly does a simple task, like adding numbers or squaring a number."

1. **Reinforcement:**

- Reinforce learning with fun activities, like creating mini spells (lambda functions) to solve small problems.
- **Example:** "Write a short story where they use lambda functions to help with different tasks, like checking if a number is big or small."

# Chapter 7 Basic Data Structures

Lists

Teaching Lists
Objective: Help young children understand and use lists in Python through engaging examples and activities.

1. **Introduction to Lists:**

- Explain that lists are collections of items, like a treasure chest filled with toys, candies, or anything they like.
- **Example:** "Lists are like magic treasure chests that can hold lots of treasures (items) inside them."

1. **Creating a List:**

- Show how to create a list using square brackets [] and separate items with commas.

- **Example:** "Type favorite_fruits = ["apple", "banana", "cherry"] to create a list of favorite fruits."

1. **Accessing Items in a List:**

- Show how to get items from a list using their position (index).
- **Example:** "Type first_fruit = favorite_fruits[0] to get the first item from the list."

1. **Adding Items to a List:**

- Show how to add items to a list using the append method.
- **Example:** "Type favorite_fruits.append("orange") to add an item to the list."

1. **Removing Items from a List:**

- Show how to remove items from a list using the remove method.
- **Example:** "Type favorite_fruits.remove("banana") to remove an item from the list."

1. **Hands-On Practice:**

- Encourage the children to create their own lists and practice adding, removing, and accessing items.
- **Example:** "Type favorite_animals = ["cat", "dog", "elephant"] to create a list of favorite animals and practice adding, removing, and accessing items."

1. **Interactive Exploration:**

- Provide simple tasks for the children to practice using lists.
- **Example:** "Create a list of their favorite toys and play with adding, removing, and accessing items."

1. **Visual Aids:**

- Use visual aids to show how lists work.
- **Example:** "Draw a picture of a treasure chest with different items inside to represent a list and show how items can be added, removed, and accessed."

1. **Reinforcement:**

- Reinforce learning with fun activities, like making stories where they use lists to keep track of items.
- **Example:** "Write a short story where they create and use lists to keep track of items in a treasure hunt."

## Tuples

**Teaching Tuples**
  **Objective: Help young children understand and use tuples in Python through engaging examples and activities.**

1. **Introduction to Tuples:**

- Explain that tuples are collections of items, like a treasure chest filled with toys, but once packed, the items inside can't be changed.

- **Example:** "Tuples are like special treasure chests that hold treasures (items) inside, but you can't change what's inside once they're packed."

1. **Creating a Tuple:**

- Show how to create a tuple using round brackets () and separate items with commas.
- **Example:** "Type favorite_colors = ("red", "blue", "green") to create a tuple of favorite colors."

1. **Accessing Items in a Tuple:**

- Show how to get items from a tuple using their position (index).
- **Example:** "Type first_color = favorite_colors[0] to get the first item from the tuple."

1. **Tuples Are Unchangeable:**

- Explain that once a tuple is created, the items inside can't be changed.
- **Example:** "Type favorite_colors[0] = "yellow" and explain why this gives an error."

1. **Hands-On Practice:**

- Encourage the children to create their own tuples and practice accessing items.

- **Example:** "Type favorite_animals = ("cat", "dog", "ele-phant") to create a tuple of favorite animals and practice accessing items."

1. **Interactive Exploration:**

- Provide simple tasks for the children to practice using tuples.
- **Example:** "Create a tuple of their favorite toys and play with accessing items."

1. **Visual Aids:**

- Use visual aids to show how tuples work.
- **Example:** "Draw a picture of a sealed treasure chest with different items inside to represent a tuple and show how items can be accessed but not changed."

1. **Reinforcement:**

- Reinforce learning with fun activities, like making stories where they use tuples to keep track of items.
- **Example:** "Write a short story where they create and use tuples to keep track of items in a sealed treasure chest."

## Sets

**Teaching Sets**
**Objective: Help young children understand and use sets in Python through engaging examples and activities.**

1. **Introduction to Sets:**

- Explain that sets are collections of unique items, like a magic box that won't allow any two toys to be the same.
- **Example:** "Sets are like magical collections that make sure there are no duplicates and keep everything unique."

1. **Creating a Set:**

- Show how to create a set using curly braces {} and separate items with commas.
- **Example:** "Type favorite_colors = {"red", "blue", "green"} to create a set of favorite colors."

1. **Adding Items to a Set:**

- Show how to add items to a set using the add method.
- **Example:** "Type favorite_colors.add("yellow") to add an item to the set."

1. **Removing Items from a Set:**

- Show how to remove items from a set using the remove method.
- **Example:** "Type favorite_colors.remove("blue") to re-

move an item from the set."

1. **No Duplicates Allowed:**

- Explain that sets don't allow duplicate items.
- **Example:** "Type favorite_colors.add("red") to add a duplicate item and explain why it only keeps one."

1. **Hands-On Practice:**

- Encourage the children to create their own sets and practice adding, removing, and checking for duplicates.
- **Example:** "Type favorite_animals = {"cat", "dog", "elephant"} to create a set of favorite animals and practice adding, removing, and checking for duplicates."

1. **Interactive Exploration:**

- Provide simple tasks for the children to practice using sets.
- **Example:** "Create a set of their favorite toys and play with adding, removing, and checking for duplicates."

1. **Visual Aids:**

- Use visual aids to show how sets work.
- **Example:** "Draw a picture of a magic box that only keeps unique items to represent a set and show how items can be added, removed, and checked for duplicates."

1. **Reinforcement:**

- Reinforce learning with fun activities, like making stories where they use sets to keep track of unique items.
- **Example:** "Write a short story where they create and use sets to keep track of unique items in a magic collection."

## Dictionaries

**Teaching Dictionaries**
   **Objective: Help young children understand and use dictionaries in Python through engaging examples and activities.**

1. **Introduction to Dictionaries:**

- Explain that dictionaries are collections of pairs, like a magical book where each word (key) has a special meaning (value).
- **Example:** "Dictionaries are like magical books that store pairs of words and their meanings, but we call them keys and values."

1. **Creating a Dictionary:**

- Show how to create a dictionary using curly braces {} and separate pairs with commas. Each pair has a key and a value separated by a colon :.
- **Example:** "Type favorite_fruits = {"apple": "red", "banana": "yellow", "grape": "purple"} to create a dictionary of favorite fruits and their colors."

1. **Accessing Values in a Dictionary:**

- Show how to get the value (meaning) from a dictionary using the key (word).
- **Example:** "Type apple_color = favorite_fruits["apple"] to get the value for the key 'apple'."

1. **Adding Items to a Dictionary:**

- Show how to add more pairs to a dictionary by assigning a value to a new key.
- **Example:** "Type favorite_fruits["orange"] = "orange" to add a new pair to the dictionary."

1. **Removing Items from a Dictionary:**

- Show how to remove pairs from a dictionary using the del keyword.
- **Example:** "Type del favorite_fruits["banana"] to remove a pair from the dictionary."

1. **Hands-On Practice:**

- Encourage the children to create their own dictionaries and practice accessing values, adding, and removing pairs.
- **Example:** "Type favorite_animals = {"cat": "meow", "dog": "woof", "cow": "moo"} to create a dictionary of favorite animals and their sounds and practice accessing values, adding, and removing pairs."

1. **Interactive Exploration:**

- Provide simple tasks for the children to practice using dictionaries.
- **Example:** "Create a dictionary of their favorite toys and their colors and play with accessing values, adding, and removing pairs."

1. **Visual Aids:**

- Use visual aids to show how dictionaries work.
- **Example:** "Draw a picture of a magical book with words and their meanings to represent a dictionary and show how pairs can be added, accessed, and removed."

1. **Reinforcement:**

- Reinforce learning with fun activities, like making stories where they use dictionaries to keep track of pairs.
- **Example:** "Write a short story where they create and use dictionaries to keep track of pairs in a magical book."

# 11

# Input and Output(chapter 7)

- Reading from and writing to the console

Teaching Reading from and Writing to the Console Objective: Help young children understand and use the console in Python through engaging examples and activities.

## Introduction to the Console:

- Explain that the console is like a special chat window where they can see messages from the computer and send messages to it.
- **Example:** "The console is like a magical notebook where you can write things and your computer can write back."

1. **Writing to the Console:**

- Show how to use the print function to write messages to

the console.

- **Example:** "Type print("Hello, computer!") to write a message to the console."

1. **Reading from the Console:**

- Show how to use the input function to read messages from the console.
- **Example:** "Type name = input("What is your name? ") to read a message from the console and store it in a variable."

1. **Combining Reading and Writing:**

- Show how to combine input and print to create interactive messages.
- **Example:** "Type name = input("What is your name? ") and print("Hello, " + name + "!") to create an interactive greeting."

1. **Hands-On Practice:**

- Encourage the children to create their own interactive messages and practice reading and writing to the console.
- **Example:** "Type favorite_color = input("What is your favorite color? ") and print("Wow! " + favorite_color + " is a beautiful color!") to create an interactive color message."

1. **Fun with Numbers:**

- Show how to read numbers from the console and perform simple arithmetic.

- **Example:** "Type number1 = int(input("Enter the first number: ")) and number2 = int(input("Enter the second number: ")) to read numbers and perform addition."

1. **Interactive Exploration:**

- Provide simple tasks for the children to practice reading from and writing to the console.
- **Example:** "Create a game where they ask for their favorite animal and make it say something, like favorite_animal = input("What is your favorite animal? ") and print("The " + favorite_animal + " says hello!")."

1. **Visual Aids:**

- Use visual aids to show how the console works.
- **Example:** "Draw a picture of a magical chat window to represent the console and show how messages can be written and read."

1. **Reinforcement:**

- Reinforce learning with fun activities, like making stories where they use the console to create interactive messages.
- **Example:** "Write a short story where they create and use the console to create interactive messages in a magical chat window."

# File handling (read, write, append)

**For Teachers:**

**Teaching File Handling: Reading, Writing, and Appending**
  **Objective:** Help young children understand and use file handling in Python through engaging examples and activities.

1. **Introduction to Files:**

- Explain that files are like magical notebooks where they can write down things and read them later.
- **Example:** "A file is like a magical notebook where you can write stories, notes, or anything you want and read it anytime."

1. **Reading from a File:**

- Show how to open a file and read its contents using the open and read functions.
- **Example:** "Type file = open("story.txt", "r"), story = file.read(), and file.close() to read from a file."

1. **Writing to a File:**

- Show how to open a file and write new contents using the open and write functions.
- **Example:** "Type file = open("mystory.txt", "w") and file.write("Once upon a time…") to write to a file."

1. **Appending to a File:**

- Show how to open a file and add more contents without erasing the old ones using the open and append functions.
- **Example:** "Type file = open("mystory.txt", "a") and file.write("More story…") to append to a file."

1. **Hands-On Practice:**

- Encourage the children to create their own files and practice reading from, writing to, and appending to them.
- **Example:** "Create a file called notes.txt, write notes inside, and practice reading and appending to it."

1. **Interactive Exploration:**

- Provide simple tasks for the children to practice file handling.
- **Example:** "Write a short story into a file, read it, and then add more to the story and read the updated story."

1. **Visual Aids:**

- Use visual aids to show how file handling works.
- **Example:** "Draw a picture of a magical notebook to represent a file and show how contents can be written, read, and appended."

1. **Reinforcement:**

- Reinforce learning with fun activities, like making stories where they use file handling to create and update magical notebooks.

- **Example:** "Write a short story into a file, read it, add more to the story, and read the updated story to create and update magical notebooks."

# 12

# Level 2 Intermediate

# Chapter 8 Advanced Data Structures

List comprehensions

Teaching Advanced Data Structures: List Comprehensions

Objective: Help young children understand and use list comprehensions in Python through engaging examples and activities.

1. **Introduction to List Comprehensions:**

- Explain that list comprehensions are a special and easy way to create lists.
- **Example:** "Imagine you have a magical wand that can create lists in a super quick way. That's what list comprehensions do!"

1. **Creating Simple Lists:**

- Show how to create a simple list of numbers using a list comprehension.
- **Example:** "Type numbers = [x for x in range(1, 6)] to create a list of numbers from 1 to 5."

1. **Creating Lists of Squares:**

- Show how to create a list of squares of numbers using a list comprehension.
- **Example:** "Type squares = [x * x for x in range(1, 6)] to create a list of squares of numbers from 1 to 5."

1. **Creating Lists of Even Numbers:**

- Show how to create a list of even numbers using a list comprehension.
- **Example:** "Type even_numbers = [x for x in range(1, 11) if x % 2 == 0] to create a list of even numbers from 1 to 10."

1. **Creating Lists of First Letters:**

- Show how to create a list of the first letters of words using a list comprehension.
- **Example:** "Type words = ["apple", "banana", "cherry"] and first_letters = [word[0] for word in words] to create a list of the first letters of the words."

1. **Combining Lists:**

- Show how to combine two lists into one using a list

comprehension.
- **Example:** "Type fruits = ["apple", "banana"] and colors = ["red", "yellow"] to combine the lists into fruit_colors = [fruit + " is " + color for fruit, color in zip(fruits, colors)]."

1. **Hands-On Practice:**

- Encourage the children to create their own lists using list comprehensions.
- **Example:** "Create a list of your favorite animals and their sounds using a list comprehension."

1. **Interactive Exploration:**

- Provide simple tasks for the children to practice using list comprehensions.
- **Example:** "Create a list of your favorite things and use list comprehensions to make magical lists."

1. **Visual Aids:**

- Use visual aids to show how list comprehensions work.
- **Example:** "Draw pictures of magical wands creating lists to represent how list comprehensions work."

1. **Reinforcement:**

- Reinforce learning with fun activities, like creating and using list comprehensions to make magical lists of favorite things.
- **Example:** "Write a short story using list comprehensions

to create and update lists of characters and their actions."

## Dictionary comprehensions

**Teaching Advanced Data Structures: Dictionary Comprehensions**

**Objective: Help young children understand and use dictionary comprehensions in Python through engaging examples and activities.**

1. **Introduction to Dictionary Comprehensions:**

- Explain that dictionary comprehensions are a special and easy way to create dictionaries.
- **Example:** "Imagine you have a magical book that has pairs of things. Each pair has a key and a value, like a name and a favorite color."

1. **Creating Simple Dictionaries:**

- Show how to create a simple dictionary using a dictionary comprehension.
- **Example:** "Type squares = {x: x * x for x in range(1, 6)} to create a dictionary where the keys are numbers from 1 to 5, and the values are their squares."

1. **Creating Dictionaries of Lengths:**

- Show how to create a dictionary where the keys are names and the values are the lengths of those names.
- **Example:** "Type names = ["Alice", "Bob", "Charlie"] and name_lengths = {name: len(name) for name in names} to create a dictionary where the keys are names and the values are the lengths of the names."

1. **Creating Dictionaries of Favorite Fruits:**

- Show how to create a dictionary where the keys are names and the values are their favorite fruits.
- **Example:** "Type names = ["Alice", "Bob", "Charlie"] and favorite_fruits = ["apple", "banana", "cherry"] to create a dictionary using fruits_dict = {name: fruit for name, fruit in zip(names, favorite_fruits)}."

1. **Creating Dictionaries of Even and Odd Numbers:**

- Show how to create a dictionary where the keys are numbers from 1 to 10 and the values are "even" or "odd".
- **Example:** "Type even_odd = {x: "even" if x % 2 == 0 else "odd" for x in range(1, 11)} to create a dictionary where the keys are numbers from 1 to 10 and the values are 'even' or 'odd'."

1. **Hands-On Practice:**

- Encourage the children to create their own dictionaries using dictionary comprehensions.
- **Example:** "Create a dictionary of your favorite animals and their sounds using a dictionary comprehension."

1. **Interactive Exploration:**

- Provide simple tasks for the children to practice using dictionary comprehensions.
- **Example:** "Create a dictionary of your favorite things and use dictionary comprehensions to make magical dictionaries."

1. **Visual Aids:**

- Use visual aids to show how dictionary comprehensions work.
- **Example:** "Draw pictures of magical books creating pairs of things to represent how dictionary comprehensions work."

1. **Reinforcement:**

- Reinforce learning with fun activities, like creating and using dictionary comprehensions to make magical dictionaries of favorite things.
- **Example:** "Write a short story using dictionary comprehensions to create and update dictionaries of characters and their actions."

## Nested data structures

**For Teachers:**

**Teaching Advanced Data Structures: Nested Data Structures**
  **Objective: Help young children understand and use nested data structures in Python through engaging examples and activities.**

1. **Introduction to Nested Data Structures:**

- Explain that nested data structures are like having containers inside other containers.
- **Example:** "Imagine you have a big box with smaller boxes inside it. Each smaller box can also have even smaller boxes inside it. That's what nested data structures are!"

1. **Creating Nested Lists:**

- Show how to create a list inside another list.
- **Example:** "Type toys = [["red car", "blue bike"], ["yellow truck", "green boat"]] to create a list of lists, where each sublist has different types of toys."

1. **Accessing Nested Lists:**

- Demonstrate how to access elements in a nested list.
- **Example:** "Type print(toys[0]) to see the first list of

toys. To see the second toy in the second list, type print(toys[1][1])."

1. **Creating Nested Dictionaries:**

• Show how to create a dictionary inside another dictionary.
• **Example:** "Type book = { "Chapter 1": {"Page 1": "Introduction", "Page 2": "Getting Started"}, "Chapter 2": {"Page 1": "Advanced Topics", "Page 2": "Conclusion"}} to create a dictionary with chapters and pages."

1. **Accessing Nested Dictionaries:**

• Demonstrate how to access elements in a nested dictionary.
• **Example:** "Type print(book["Chapter 1"]["Page 2"]) to see what's on Page 2 of Chapter 1."

1. **Combining Nested Lists and Dictionaries:**

• Show how to combine lists and dictionaries to create more complex structures.
• **Example:** "Type people = [{"Name": "Alice", "Favorites": {"Color": "blue", "Animal": "cat"}},{"Name": "Bob", "Favorites": {"Color": "green", "Animal": "dog"}}] to create a list of people with dictionaries for their favorite things."

1. **Accessing Combined Structures:**

• Demonstrate how to access elements in combined nested structures.

73

- **Example:** "Type print(people[0]["Favorites"]["Animal"]) to see what Alice's favorite animal is."

1. **Hands-On Practice:**

- Encourage children to create their own nested data structures with lists and dictionaries.
- **Example:** "Create a list of your favorite things and use nested dictionaries to add details about each item."

1. **Interactive Exploration:**

- Provide simple tasks for the children to practice using nested data structures.
- **Example:** "Create a nested data structure that describes a fun day at the park with details about different activities."

1. **Visual Aids:**

- Use visual aids to show how nested data structures work.
- **Example:** "Draw pictures of boxes inside boxes to represent nested lists and dictionaries."

1. **Reinforcement:**

- Reinforce learning with fun activities, like creating and exploring nested data structures with favorite things and details.
- **Example:** "Write a short story using nested data structures to describe a magical adventure with favorite characters and their special traits."

1. **Modules and Packages**

# Importing modules

**Teaching Modules and Packages: Importing Modules**
  Objective: Help young children understand how to import and use modules in Python through engaging examples and activities.

1. **Introduction to Modules:**

- Explain that modules are like special treasure chests filled with pre-written code (spells) that can make coding easier and more fun.
- **Example:** "Imagine you have a treasure chest with magic spells that you can use in your coding adventures."

1. **Importing a Module:**

- Show how to import a module to use its features.
- **Example:** "Type import math to open the math module treasure chest. It contains magic spells for math!"

1. **Using Functions from Imported Modules:**

- Demonstrate how to use functions from an imported module.
- **Example:** "Type import math and then use math.sqrt(16) to find the square root of 16. The result will be 4.0."

1. **Exploring Different Modules:**

- Introduce other modules, such as random, and show how to use them.
- **Example:** "Type import random and use random.randint(1, 10) to get a random number between 1 and 10."

1. **Creating and Importing Custom Modules:**

- Show how to create a custom module and use it in another Python file.
- **Example:** "Create a file named my_magic.py with a function say_hello(). Import it in another file and use my_magic.say_hello()."

1. **Hands-On Practice:**

- Encourage children to create their own modules with simple functions and use them.
- **Example:** "Create a module with a fun function and use it in your Python programs."

1. **Interactive Exploration:**

- Provide activities where children can import and use different modules to solve simple problems or create fun projects.
- **Example:** "Import the random module and create a simple game that uses random numbers."

1. **Visual Aids:**

- Use visual aids to show how importing modules works.
- **Example:** "Draw a treasure chest filled with code snippets to represent a module."

1. **Reinforcement:**

- Reinforce learning with fun activities, like creating and using custom modules for games or stories.
- **Example:** "Create a module with magic spells for a storytelling game and use them in your stories."

## Creating and using packages

**Teaching Creating and Using Packages: Organizing Code with Packages**
**Objective: Help young children understand how to create and use packages in Python through engaging examples and activities.**

1. **Introduction to Packages:**

- Explain that packages are like large containers that can hold multiple modules (smaller containers) to keep code organized.
- **Example:** "Imagine a package as a big toy box that contains smaller boxes with different toys (modules) inside."

1. **Creating a Package:**

- Guide children through creating a package with a folder and a special file.
- **Steps:**

1. **Create a Folder:**

- Have children create a new folder named my_package.

1. **Add __init__.py:**

- Inside my_package, create a file named __init__.py to mark it as a package.

1. **Add Modules:**

- Create additional Python files within my_package, such as toys.py, to hold different functions.

1. **Adding Code to Modules:**

- Show how to write simple functions in modules.
- **Example:** "In toys.py, write a function like def get_toy(): return 'Magic Wand'."

1. **Using the Package:**

- Demonstrate how to import and use the package in a main script.
- **Example:**

import my_package.toys

```
toy = my_package.toys.get_toy()
  print(toy) # Output: Magic Wand
```

1. **Expanding the Package:**

- Encourage creating more modules within the package.
- **Example:** "Add a games.py module with more fun functions and use them in your main script."

1. **Creating a Coding Playground:**

- Help children build a collection of modules in their package for various coding activities.
- **Example:** Create a package with multiple modules for different types of games or stories.

1. **Interactive Activities:**

- Provide activities where children create and use their own packages.
- **Example:** "Have children build a package with their favorite functions and use them in a project."

1. **Visual Aids:**

- Use diagrams to illustrate how packages and modules are organized.
- **Example:** "Draw a big box (package) with smaller boxes (modules) inside to show the structure."

1. **Reinforcement:**

- Reinforce learning with fun projects that involve creating and using packages.
- **Example:** "Create a package for a storytelling game with different modules for characters, settings, and plots."

## Python Standard Library

**Teaching the Python Standard Library: An Overview of Useful Tools**
  **Objective: Help young children understand how to use the Python Standard Library by introducing key modules with simple explanations and engaging examples.**

1. **Introduction to the Python Standard Library:**

- Explain that the Python Standard Library is a collection of pre-written modules (tools) that come with Python. These modules provide ready-to-use functions and classes for various tasks.
- **Analogy:** "Think of the Standard Library as a big toolbox full of different tools that can help you with many coding tasks."

1. **Importing Modules:**

- Show how to import modules from the Standard Library to use their features.
- **Example:**

import random

1. **Key Modules and Examples:**

- **Module 1: random**
- This module provides functions for generating random numbers and choices.
- **Example:**

```
import random
number = random.randint(1, 10)
print(number) # Output: A random number between 1 and 10
```

- **Activity:** Create a simple game where students guess a randomly generated number.
- **Module 2: math**
- This module provides mathematical functions, such as calculating square roots and trigonometric functions.
- **Example:**

```
import math
square_root = math.sqrt(25)
print(square_root) # Output: 5.0
```

- **Activity:** Use math to solve simple math problems or create math-based games.
- **Module 3: datetime**
- This module helps with working with dates and times.
- **Example:**

```
import datetime
  today = datetime.date.today()
  print(today) # Output: The current date
```

- **Activity:** Use datetime to display the current date and time or calculate days between two dates.
- **Module 4: os**
- This module provides functions for interacting with the operating system, such as file and directory manipulation.
- **Example:**

```
import os
  print(os.getcwd()) # Output: The current working directory
```

- **Activity:** Use os to list files in a directory or create new folders.

1. **Hands-On Projects:**

- Encourage students to create simple projects using these modules.
- **Example:** Build a guessing game using the random module or a calendar app using datetime.

1. **Exploring More Modules:**

- Highlight that the Standard Library includes many more modules for different tasks. Encourage exploration and experimentation.
- **Activity:** Provide a list of additional modules (e.g., json, requests) and have students explore their functionality.

1. **Interactive Exploration:**

- Use interactive exercises and activities to reinforce learning.
- **Example:** Create a scavenger hunt where students use different modules to find and solve clues.

1. **Visual Aids:**

- Use diagrams or charts to illustrate how different modules can be used in coding projects.
- **Example:** Create a visual representation of a toolbox with labeled tools (modules) and their uses.

1. **Reinforcement:**

- Reinforce learning with regular practice and projects that utilize various modules from the Standard Library.
- **Example:** Assign a project where students must use multiple modules to build a comprehensive application.

# 14

# chapter 10 Exception Handling

Try, except blocks

Teaching Exception Handling: Using Try and Except Blocks
Objective: Help young children understand how to handle errors in their code using try and except blocks.

1. **Introduction to Exceptions:**

- Explain that exceptions are errors that occur when the code doesn't work as expected.
- **Analogy:** "Imagine a toy car that sometimes doesn't work because it's out of batteries. This is like an exception in code."

1. **Explaining Try and Except Blocks:**

- Introduce the concept of using try to run code that might cause an error and except to handle the error if it occurs.
- **Example:**

```
try:
  result = 10 / 2
  print(result) # Output: 5.0
except ZeroDivisionError:
  print("Oops! You can't divide by zero!")
```

1. **Detailed Explanation:**

- **Try Block:**
- This is where you write code that might cause an exception.
- **Example:** try: result = 10 / number
- **Except Block:**
- This is where you handle the exception if it occurs.
- **Example:** except ZeroDivisionError: print("Oops! You can't divide by zero!")

1. **Interactive Examples:**

- **Example 1: Basic Exception Handling**

```
try:
  number = int(input("Enter a number: "))
  result = 10 / number
  print("The result is:", result)
except ValueError:
  print("Oops! That's not a number!")
```

except ZeroDivisionError:
print("Oops! You can't divide by zero!")

- **Example 2: Handling Multiple Exceptions**
- Show how to handle different types of exceptions with multiple except blocks.

1. **Hands-On Activities:**

- Create coding exercises where students practice handling different exceptions.
- **Activity:** Build a simple calculator that catches and handles division by zero and input errors.

1. **Visual Aids:**

- Use diagrams or flowcharts to illustrate how try and except blocks work.
- **Example:** Draw a flowchart showing the flow of code through try and except blocks.

1. **Reinforcement:**

- Reinforce the concept with regular practice and debugging exercises.
- **Activity:** Provide students with code that contains intentional errors and have them use try and except to fix the issues.

1. **Exploring Further:**

- Introduce the finally and else clauses for more advanced exception handling.
- **Example:**

```
try:
  result = 10 / 2
  except ZeroDivisionError:
  print("Oops! You can't divide by zero!")
  else:
  print("No errors, result is:", result)
  finally:
  print("This will always run.")
```

This will be covered more on the next topic

**This approach helps students understand how to anticipate and handle errors, making their coding experience smoother and more enjoyable.**

## Finally and else clauses

**Teaching Finally and Else Clauses in Exception Handling**
**Objective: Help young children understand how to use the finally and else clauses to enhance exception handling in their code.**

1. **Introduction to Finally and Else:**

- Explain that finally and else are additional parts of exception handling that help ensure code runs smoothly and always performs cleanup.

- **Analogy:** "Think of finally as the cleanup crew that always arrives to tidy up, and else as a celebration for when everything works perfectly."

1. **Using Finally Clause:**

- The finally clause always executes, regardless of whether an exception occurred or not.
- **Example:**

```python
Copy code
try:
print("Trying to divide numbers.")
result = 10 / 2
print("The result is:", result)
except ZeroDivisionError:
print("Oops! You can't divide by zero!")
finally:
print("This message always shows up!")
```

- **Explanation:** "The finally block is useful for code that must run no matter what, such as closing files or releasing resources."

1. **Using Else Clause:**

- The else clause runs only if the try block executes without raising an exception.
- **Example:**

python
Copy code

```python
try:
print("Trying to divide numbers.")
result = 10 / 2
print("The result is:", result)
except ZeroDivisionError:
print("Oops! You can't divide by zero!")
else:
print("Everything worked perfectly!")
```

- **Explanation:** "The else block is great for code that should run only if no errors occur, such as reporting success."

1. **Combining Finally and Else:**

- Show how both finally and else can be used together to ensure code works correctly and always performs cleanup.
- **Example:**

```python
try:
number = int(input("Enter a number: "))
result = 10 / number
print("The result is:", result)
except ValueError:
print("Oops! That's not a number!")
except ZeroDivisionError:
print("Oops! You can't divide by zero!")
else:
print("Everything worked perfectly!")
finally:
```

print("This message always shows up!")

- **Explanation:** "Using both finally and else ensures your code handles exceptions gracefully and always performs necessary cleanup."

1. **Hands-On Activities:**

- **Activity 1:** Create exercises where students write code that uses finally to ensure resources are cleaned up, such as closing files.
- **Activity 2:** Write scenarios where students use else to celebrate successful execution of code without errors.

1. **Visual Aids:**

- Use flowcharts to show how try, except, else, and finally work together.
- **Example:** Create a flowchart that illustrates the flow of code through these blocks.

1. **Reinforcement:**

- Practice with multiple examples and scenarios to reinforce understanding.
- **Activity:** Provide code with intentional errors and ask students to handle exceptions using finally and else.

1. **Exploring Further:**

- Discuss real-world examples where finally and else are

useful, such as managing files or network connections.

**This approach helps students understand and effectively use finally and else to handle exceptions and ensure their code runs smoothly.**

## Custom exceptions

**Teaching Custom Exceptions: Creating and Using Your Own Exception Types**

  Objective: **Help young children understand how to create and use custom exceptions to handle specific errors in their code.**

  *I would recommend you skip this part and come back to it after teaching your student about classes which is our next lesson*

1. **Introduction to Custom Exceptions:**

   - Explain that custom exceptions are user-defined error types that help handle specific situations in code. They allow you to create more meaningful and tailored error messages.
   - **Analogy:** "Custom exceptions are like making your own special rules for when things go wrong in your code."

1. **Creating a Custom Exception Class:**

   - Teach students to create a custom exception by defining a new class that inherits from the built-in Exception class.

- **Example:**

```
class MyCustomError(Exception):
    def __init__(self, message):
    self.message = message
    super().__init__(self.message)
```

- **Explanation:** "You create a new class for your custom exception, add an __init__ method to pass a message, and use super() to initialize the base class."

1. **Using Custom Exceptions:**

- Show how to raise and handle custom exceptions using try and except blocks.
- **Example:**

```
try:
    raise MyCustomError("Something went wrong!")
    except MyCustomError as e:
    print("Custom Exception caught:", e)
```

- **Explanation:** "Use the raise keyword to trigger your custom exception and except to catch and handle it."

1. **Interactive Examples:**

- **Example 1:** Create a simple program where custom exceptions are used to handle specific errors.

```
class TooHighError(Exception):
```

```
def __init__(self, message):
    self.message = message
    super().__init__(self.message)

number = int(input("Guess a number between 1 and 10: "))

try:
    if number > 10:
    raise TooHighError("Oops! That number is too high!")
    print("You guessed:", number)
    except TooHighError as e:
    print(e)
```

- **Example 2:** Provide scenarios where custom exceptions can be used to enforce specific rules or constraints.

1. **Hands-On Activities:**

- **Activity 1:** Have students create their own custom exceptions for different scenarios or games.
- **Activity 2:** Practice raising and handling custom exceptions in various coding exercises.

1. **Visual Aids:**

- Use diagrams to illustrate how custom exceptions fit into the try and except blocks.
- **Example:** Draw a flowchart showing the creation and handling of custom exceptions.

1. **Reinforcement:**

- Regularly practice creating and using custom exceptions to reinforce understanding.
- **Activity:** Provide coding challenges where students need to use custom exceptions to handle specific situations.

1. **Exploring Further:**

- Discuss how custom exceptions can be used in larger projects to create more readable and maintainable code.

**This approach helps students grasp the concept of custom exceptions and effectively use them to handle specific errors in their programs.**

# chapter 11 Object-Oriented Programming (OOP)

## Classes and objects

Teaching Object-Oriented Programming: Classes and Objects
Objective: Help young children understand the concepts of classes and objects in programming, focusing on the basic idea of self to personalize objects.

1. **Introduction to Classes and Objects:**

- Explain that classes are like blueprints or recipes for creating objects, while objects are the actual instances created from those blueprints.
- **Analogy:** "A class is like a toy factory that has instructions for making toys, and an object is one of the toys made from those instructions."

1. **Creating a Class:**

- Start by defining a simple class with an __init__ method to initialize object properties.
- **Example:**

```
class ToyRobot:
    def __init__(self, name):
    self.name = name

def say_hello(self):
    print(f"Hello! I am {self.name} the robot!")
```

- **Explanation:** "The __init__ method sets up the robot's name, and the say_hello method makes the robot introduce itself."

1. **Understanding Self:**

- Explain that self refers to the object itself and helps the object remember its own details and behaviors.
- **Analogy:** "Think of self as the robot's name tag. It tells the robot who it is and helps it use its special features."

1. **Creating and Using Objects:**

- Show how to create an object from a class and use its methods.
- **Example:**

python

```
Copy code
# Create a toy robot
my_robot = ToyRobot("RoboBuddy")
```

```
# Make the robot say hello
my_robot.say_hello()
```

- **Explanation:** "We create a robot called RoboBuddy and use the say_hello method to make it introduce itself."

1. **Interactive Example:**

- **Example 1:** Create a class for a magical wand.

python
```
Copy code
class MagicWand:
def __init__(self, color):
self.color = color
```

```
def cast_spell(self):
    print(f"Swish and flick! The {self.color} wand casts a spell!")
```

- **Creating and Using the Wand:**

```
my_wand = MagicWand("blue")
my_wand.cast_spell()
```

- **Explanation:** "The blue wand uses its special cast_spell method to perform magic."

1. **Hands-On Activities:**

- **Activity 1:** Have students create their own classes for different objects, such as pets or vehicles.
- **Activity 2:** Let students design objects with different properties and methods, exploring how self is used to manage these details.

1. **Visual Aids:**

- Use diagrams to illustrate the relationship between classes and objects.
- **Example:** Create a flowchart showing how a class defines the structure and how objects use this structure.

1. **Reinforcement:**

- Practice creating classes and objects through various coding exercises and projects.
- **Activity:** Provide scenarios where students need to define classes and create objects to solve specific problems.

1. **Exploring Further:**

- Discuss how classes and objects are used in larger projects to organize and manage code.

**This approach helps students grasp the foundational concepts of classes and objects and understand how self personalizes each object.**

## Methods and attributes

**Teaching Object-Oriented Programming: Methods and Attributes**

Objective: Help young children understand the concepts of methods and attributes within object-oriented programming, focusing on their roles and how they enhance objects.

1. **Introduction to Attributes:**

- Explain that attributes are the properties or characteristics of an object, describing what it is like.
- **Analogy:** "Attributes are like the features or traits of a toy. For example, a toy robot's color and name are its attributes."

1. **Creating Attributes:**

- Show how to define attributes in the __init__ method of a class.
- **Example:**

```
class ToyRobot:
    def __init__(self, name, color):
    self.name = name
    self.color = color
```

- **Explanation:** "In this example, name and color are

99

attributes of the ToyRobot class. self.name and self.color store these values."

1. **Introduction to Methods:**

- Explain that methods are functions defined inside a class that describe what the object can do.
- **Analogy:** "Methods are like the actions or tricks that a toy can perform. For example, a toy robot can say hello or dance."

1. **Creating Methods:**

- Show how to define methods within a class to perform actions or provide information.
- **Example:**

```
class ToyRobot:
    def __init__(self, name, color):
    self.name = name
    self.color = color
```

```
def say_hello(self):
    print(f"Hello! I am {self.name} and I am {self.color}!")
```

- **Explanation:** "The say_hello method makes the toy robot introduce itself using its name and color attributes."

1. **Interactive Example:**

- **Example 1:** Create a class for a magical wand with

100

attributes and methods.

```
class MagicWand:
    def __init__(self, color, power):
    self.color = color
    self.power = power

def cast_spell(self):
    print(f"Swish and flick!    The {self.color} wand with
{self.power} power casts a spell!")
```

- **Creating and Using the Wand:**

```
my_wand = MagicWand("green", "flying")
    my_wand.cast_spell()
```

- **Explanation:** "The wand has attributes color and power, and the cast_spell method describes what the wand does."

1. **Hands-On Activities:**

- **Activity 1:** Have students create their own classes with attributes and methods for different objects, such as pets or vehicles.
- **Activity 2:** Practice using attributes and methods in coding exercises where students create objects with various features and actions.

1. **Visual Aids:**

- Use diagrams to illustrate how attributes and methods are

101

defined and used in a class.
- **Example:** Create a chart showing the relationship between attributes, methods, and objects.

1. **Reinforcement:**

- Reinforce understanding through practice exercises where students define attributes and methods for different scenarios.
- **Activity:** Provide coding challenges where students need to create classes with meaningful attributes and methods.

1. **Exploring Further:**

- Discuss how attributes and methods are used in larger projects to organize and manage code effectively.

**This approach helps students understand how attributes and methods enhance the functionality of objects and how to implement them effectively in their code.**

## Inheritance

**Teaching Object-Oriented Programming: Inheritance
Objective: Help young children understand the concept of inheritance in object-oriented programming, using simple examples and analogies.**

1. **Introduction to Inheritance:**

- Explain that inheritance allows us to create new classes based on existing classes, inheriting their attributes and methods, and adding new features.
- **Analogy:** "Inheritance is like having a superhero parent who gives you special powers. You get all their cool abilities and maybe add some new ones of your own."

1. **Creating a Base Class:**

- Define a simple base class with essential attributes and methods.
- **Example:**

```
class Superhero:
   def __init__(self, name):
   self.name = name
```

```
def fly(self):
   print(f"{self.name} is flying through the sky!")
```

- **Explanation:** "The Superhero class has a name attribute and a fly method that all superheroes can use."

1. **Creating a Derived Class:**

- Show how to create a new class that inherits from the base class and adds new features.
- **Example:**

```
class SuperheroWithStrength(Superhero):
   def __init__(self, name, strength):
```

103

```
super().__init__(name)
self.strength = strength
```

```
def show_strength(self):
  print(f"{self.name} has super strength of {self.strength}!")
```

- **Explanation:** "The SuperheroWithStrength class inherits the fly method from Superhero and adds a new show_strength method."

1. **Interactive Example:**

- **Example 1:** Create a base class for a magic wand and a derived class with additional magical powers.

```
class MagicWand:
  def __init__(self, color):
  self.color = color
```

```
def wave(self):
  print(f"The {self.color} wand waves and sparkles!")
```

```
class MagicWandWithPower(MagicWand):
  def __init__(self, color, power):
  super().__init__(color)
  self.power = power
```

```
def show_power(self):
  print(f"The {self.color} wand has the power of {self.power}!")
```

- **Creating and Using the Magic Wand:**

```
enchanted_wand = MagicWandWithPower("purple", "invisi-
bility")
enchanted_wand.wave()
enchanted_wand.show_power()
```

- **Explanation:** "The MagicWandWithPower class inherits the wave method and adds a new show_power method."

1. **Hands-On Activities:**

- **Activity 1:** Have students create their own base classes and derived classes, demonstrating how inheritance works.
- **Activity 2:** Practice using inheritance in coding exercises, where students extend existing classes with new attributes and methods.

1. **Visual Aids:**

- Use diagrams to illustrate the inheritance hierarchy, showing how attributes and methods are passed down from base classes to derived classes.
- **Example:** Create a flowchart showing the relationship between base and derived classes.

1. **Reinforcement:**

- Reinforce understanding through coding exercises where students define classes, use inheritance, and explore how features are inherited and extended.

1. **Exploring Further:**

• Discuss how inheritance is used in larger projects to organize and reuse code effectively.

**This approach helps students grasp the concept of inheritance, illustrating how new classes can build on existing ones and add new features, enhancing their understanding of object-oriented programming.**

## Polymorphism

**Teaching Object-Oriented Programming: Polymorphism Objective: Help young children understand the concept of polymorphism in object-oriented programming, using simple analogies and interactive examples.**

1. **Introduction to Polymorphism:**

• Explain that polymorphism allows different classes to use the same method name, but each class can perform a different action with that method.
• **Analogy:** "Polymorphism is like having a magic wand that can do many different things depending on how you use it. Each toy can have the same button but do different tricks."

1. **Creating a Base Class:**

• Define a base class with a method that will be shared by

106

all derived classes.
- **Example:**

```
class Toy:
  def play(self):
  print("The toy is having fun!")
```

- **Explanation:** "The Toy class has a play method that can be used by all toy classes."

1. **Creating Derived Classes with Polymorphism:**

- Show how derived classes override the base class method to perform different actions.
- **Example:**

```
class DancingToy(Toy):
  def play(self):
  print("The toy is dancing!")

class SingingToy(Toy):
  def play(self):
  print("The toy is singing!")
```

- **Explanation:** "The DancingToy and SingingToy classes use the same method name play, but each toy does something different."

1. **Interactive Example:**

- **Example 1:** Create a base class for animals and derived classes for specific animals that make different sounds.

```
class Animal:
  def make_sound(self):
  print("The animal makes a sound!")

class Cat(Animal):
  def make_sound(self):
  print("The cat says meow!")

class Dog(Animal):
  def make_sound(self):
  print("The dog says woof!")
```

- **Creating and Using the Animals:**

```
my_cat = Cat()
  my_dog = Dog()

my_cat.make_sound() # Output: The cat says meow!
  my_dog.make_sound() # Output: The dog says woof!
```

- **Explanation:** "The make_sound method behaves differently depending on whether it's used with a Cat or a Dog."

1. **Hands-On Activities:**

- **Activity 1:** Have students create a base class and several derived classes that use polymorphism to perform different actions.
- **Activity 2:** Practice using polymorphism in coding exer-

cises where students define methods with the same name in different classes.

1. **Visual Aids:**

- Use diagrams to show how polymorphism allows the same method name to produce different outputs based on the class used.
- **Example:** Create a flowchart illustrating the relationship between the base class and derived classes.

1. **Reinforcement:**

- Reinforce understanding through practice exercises where students use polymorphism to enhance their projects and code.

1. **Exploring Further:**

- Discuss how polymorphism helps manage and organize code efficiently, making it easier to work with different objects that share common methods.

**This approach helps students understand how polymorphism allows different classes to use the same method name while performing different actions, enhancing their grasp of object-oriented programming concepts.**

## Encapsulation and abstraction

Teaching Object-Oriented Programming:
Encapsulation and Abstraction

**Objective: Help young children understand encapsulation and abstraction in object-oriented programming using simple explanations and interactive examples.**

## 1. Encapsulation:

- **Definition:** Encapsulation is the concept of hiding the internal details of an object and only exposing the necessary parts. It helps to keep the code organized and prevents external code from messing with internal details.
- **Analogy:** "Encapsulation is like a toy with a magic box. You can play with the toy and use its features without needing to understand how the magic box works inside."

**Example Code:**

```
class ToyRobot:
def __init__(self):
self._battery_level = 100 # Private attribute

def move(self):
  print("The robot is moving!")

def _check_battery(self): # Private method
  return self._battery_level

def play(self):
```

```
if self._check_battery() > 0:
self.move()
print("The robot is playing!")
else:
print("The robot needs new batteries!")
```

- **Explanation:** "The ToyRobot class hides its battery level and battery-checking method. We use the play method to interact with the robot without needing to worry about the battery level."

## 2. Abstraction:

- **Definition:** Abstraction is the process of hiding complex implementation details and showing only the necessary features. It simplifies the interaction with objects by providing a clear interface.
- **Analogy:** "Abstraction is like having a magic wand that can do amazing things. You don't need to know how it works; you just use it to make magic happen."

**Example Code:**
```
class MagicWand:
def wave(self):
self._cast_spell()

def _cast_spell(self): # Hidden implementation
print("The wand casts a magical spell!")
```

- **Explanation:** "The MagicWand class hides the details of how the spell is cast. You only need to use the wave method to see the magic."

## Interactive Examples:

- **Example 1:** Create a base class for a magic potion and derived classes that show how encapsulation and abstraction work.

```
class MagicPotion:
  def drink(self):
  print("You drink the potion and feel magical!")
```

```
class HealingPotion(MagicPotion):
  def __init__(self):
  self._healing_power = 50 # Hidden attribute
```

```
def use(self):
  print(f"The potion heals you by {self._healing_power} points!")
  self.drink()
```

- **Explanation:** "The HealingPotion class uses encapsulation to hide the healing power and abstraction to simplify how the potion is used."

## Hands-On Activities:

- **Activity 1:** Have students create classes that use encapsulation to hide details and abstraction to provide simple interfaces.
- **Activity 2:** Practice using encapsulation and abstraction

in coding exercises where students define classes and methods with hidden details and clear interfaces.

## Visual Aids:

- Use diagrams to illustrate how encapsulation hides internal details and how abstraction simplifies interactions with objects.

## Reinforcement:

- Reinforce understanding through practice exercises where students create classes with encapsulated details and abstracted methods.

**This approach helps students understand how encapsulation and abstraction make code easier to manage and interact with, providing clear interfaces and hiding complex details.**

# chapter 12 File Handling

## Working with different file types (text, CSV, JSON)

Teaching File Handling: Working with Different File Types

Objective: Introduce young children to file handling concepts, including text files, CSV files, and JSON files, using simple explanations and interactive examples.

1. Text Files:

- **Definition:** Text files store simple text data. They are used to save and retrieve plain text information.
- **Analogy:** "A text file is like a notebook where you write stories or notes. It keeps everything in simple text form."

**Example Code:**

```
# Writing to a text file
with open("story.txt", "w") as file:
file.write("Once upon a time, there was a magical land!")
```

```
# Reading from a text file
with open("story.txt", "r") as file:
print(file.read()) # Output: Once upon a time, there was a
magical land!
```

- **Explanation:** "We use open to create or open a file. The write method puts our story into the file, and the read method shows us what's inside."

## 2. CSV Files:

- **Definition:** CSV files store data in a table-like format with rows and columns, separated by commas. They are used for organizing and sharing tabular data.
- **Analogy:** "A CSV file is like a big table where you keep information about things, such as friends and their favorite colors."

**Example Code:**
```
import csv
```

```
# Writing to a CSV file
with open("friends.csv", "w", newline="") as file:
writer = csv.writer(file)
writer.writerow(["Name", "Favorite Color"])
writer.writerow(["Alice", "Blue"])
writer.writerow(["Bob", "Green"])
```

```
# Reading from a CSV file
  with open("friends.csv", "r") as file:
  reader = csv.reader(file)
  for row in reader:
  print(row)
```

- **Explanation:** "We use the csv module to handle CSV files. The writerow method writes rows of data, and the reader reads them back."

## 3. JSON Files:

- **Definition:** JSON files store data in a structured format that's easy for computers to read and write. It is often used for configurations and data exchange.
- **Analogy:** "A JSON file is like a super neat toy box where different toys are organized into sections. It keeps everything tidy and easy to find."

**Example Code:**
```
  import json
```

```
# Writing to a JSON file
  data = {
  "name": "Magic Toy Box",
  "toys": ["Cars", "Dolls", "Blocks"]
  }
```

```
with open("toy_box.json", "w") as file:
  json.dump(data, file)
```

```
# Reading from a JSON file
with open("toy_box.json", "r") as file:
content = json.load(file)
print(content)
```

- **Explanation:** "The json module helps us work with JSON files. The dump method saves our data, and the load method reads it back."

## Interactive Examples:

- **Example 1:** Create simple text files to store and read stories.
- **Example 2:** Use CSV files to organize and display tabular data such as a list of students or favorite foods.
- **Example 3:** Implement JSON files to store structured data like user preferences or game settings.

## Hands-On Activities:

- **Activity 1:** Have students create and manage text files for their stories or notes.
- **Activity 2:** Practice using CSV files to organize and analyze simple data sets.
- **Activity 3:** Explore JSON files to handle structured data for various applications.

## Visual Aids:

- Use diagrams to illustrate the structure of text, CSV, and JSON files.
- Show examples of how data is organized in each file type.

**This approach helps students understand the different file types and how to work with them, providing practical experience with file handling in a fun and engaging way.**

## Context managers (with statement)

Teaching File Handling: Using Context Managers with the with Statement

**Objective: Introduce young learners to the concept of context managers in file handling using simple explanations and interactive examples.**

## 1. Introduction to Context Managers:

- **Definition:** Context managers are a way to manage resources, like files, in a clean and efficient manner. They ensure that resources are properly opened and closed.
- **Analogy:** "Context managers are like having an assistant who opens and closes your file for you. This way, you don't have to worry about it."

## 2. The with Statement:

- **Purpose:** The with statement provides a convenient way to ensure that resources are properly cleaned up after use, even if errors occur.
- **Structure:**

```
with open("file.txt", "mode") as file:
    # Work with the file
```

- **Explanation:**
- open("file.txt", "mode") – Opens the file with the specified mode (e.g., "w" for writing, "r" for reading).
- as file – Assigns the opened file to the variable file.
- The file is automatically closed when the block under with is done.

## 3. Example Code:

**Writing to a File:**

```
with open("example.txt", "w") as file:
file.write("Hello, World!")
```

- **Explanation:**
- The with statement opens the file example.txt for writing.
- The file is automatically closed after the write operation is complete.

**Reading from a File:**

```
with open("example.txt", "r") as file:
```

```
content = file.read()
print(content)
```

- **Explanation:**
- The *with* statement opens the file example.txt for reading.
- The file is automatically closed after reading the content.

## 4. Benefits of Using Context Managers:

- **Automatic Cleanup:**
- Ensures that the file is properly closed after use, reducing the risk of resource leaks.
- **Simplifies Code:**
- Makes the code more readable and maintainable by managing file operations in a clear and concise manner.

## 5. Interactive Examples:

- **Example 1:** Have students use the ***with*** statement to write and read simple messages to and from a file.
- **Example 2:** Demonstrate how the file is automatically closed after the block, even if an error occurs.

## 6. Hands-On Activities:

- **Activity 1:** Create a file with student names and ages using the with statement.
- **Activity 2:** Read and display the content of the file using the with statement.

**This approach helps students understand the concept**

of context managers and the with statement, providing practical experience with file handling in a fun and engaging manner.

# Chapter 13 Iterators and Generators

Iterable objects

Teaching Iterators and Generators: Understanding
Iterable Objects

**O**bjective: **Introduce young learners to the
concept of iterable objects using simple explanations and interactive examples.**

1. Introduction to Iterable Objects:

- **Definition:** Iterable objects are collections of items that
  you can loop through one at a time. They allow you to
  access each element in a sequence.
- **Analogy:** "Iterable objects are like magical containers that
  let you access each item one by one, making it easy to go
  through the contents."

## 2. Examples of Iterable Objects:

- **Lists:**
- Lists are a common example of iterable objects. They hold a collection of items that can be accessed in sequence.
- **Example Code:**

python
```
Copy code
# Define a list of items
items = ["Apple", "Banana", "Cherry"]
```

```
# Iterate through the list
for item in items:
print(item)
```

- **Explanation:**
- items is a list (an iterable object).
- for item in items iterates through each element in the list.
- print(item) outputs each item.
- **Strings:**
- Strings are also iterable objects, where each character in the string can be accessed individually.
- **Example Code:**

python
```
Copy code
# Define a string
word = "Python"
```

```
# Iterate through the string
```

```
for char in word:
print(char)
```

- **Explanation:**
- word is a string (an iterable object).
- for char in word iterates through each character in the string.
- print(char) outputs each character.

## 3. Benefits of Iterable Objects:

- **Ease of Use:**
- Iterable objects simplify accessing and processing collections of data.
- **Versatility:**
- They can be used with various data types, including lists, strings, and more.

## 4. Interactive Examples:

- **Example 1:** Create a list of favorite fruits and iterate through it to print each fruit.
- **Example 2:** Use a string with a name or simple word and iterate through each character.

## 5. Hands-On Activities:

- **Activity 1:** Have students create their own lists of items and practice iterating through them.
- **Activity 2:** Use strings with simple words or phrases and explore iterating through each letter.

## 6. Visual Aids:

- Use diagrams to illustrate how iterable objects allow access to each element in sequence.
- Provide examples with real-world analogies like treasure boxes or ribbons.

**This approach helps students grasp the concept of iterable objects, providing practical experience with iterating through collections of items in a fun and engaging manner.**

## Creating iterators

Teaching Iterators: Creating Custom Iterators

**Objective: Introduce young learners to creating custom iterators using classes in Python, with a focus on simplicity and engagement.**

## 1. Introduction to Iterators:

- **Definition:** Iterators are objects that allow you to traverse through a collection of items one at a time. They are useful for iterating over sequences of data.
- **Analogy:** "Think of an iterator as a special tool that helps you look at each item in a list or collection, one by one, just like a toy sorter."

## 2. Creating a Custom Iterator:

- **Steps:**

1. **Define a Class:** Create a class that will act as the iterator.
2. **Initialize the Iterator:** Set up the initial state, including the items to iterate over.
3. **Implement __iter__ Method:** This method returns the iterator object itself.
4. **Implement __next__ Method:** This method returns the next item in the sequence and raises StopIteration when there are no more items.

- **Example Code:**

```python
# Define the iterator class
class ToySorter:
    def __init__(self, toys):
        self.toys = toys # List of toys
        self.index = 0 # Starting index

    def __iter__(self):
        return self # Return the iterator object

    def __next__(self):
        if self.index < len(self.toys):
            toy = self.toys[self.index] # Get the current toy
            self.index += 1 # Move to the next index
            return toy
        else:
            raise StopIteration # No more items to return
```

```
# Create an instance of the iterator
sorter = ToySorter(["Teddy Bear", "Ball", "Toy Car"])

# Iterate through the items
for toy in sorter:
print(toy)
```
**Explanation:**

- ToySorter is a custom class that acts as our iterator.
- __init__ initializes the list of items and the index.
- __iter__ returns the iterator object.
- __next__ returns the next item and handles the end of the sequence.

## 3. Benefits of Custom Iterators:

- **Control:** Provides detailed control over how items are accessed and processed.
- **Customization:** Allows for custom behavior tailored to specific needs.

## 4. Interactive Examples:

- **Example 1:** Create a simple iterator that iterates over a list of students' names.
- **Example 2:** Implement an iterator for a sequence of numbers with custom steps.

## 5. Hands-On Activities:

- **Activity 1:** Have students create a custom iterator for a list of their favorite things.
- **Activity 2:** Implement an iterator that counts down from a given number.

## 6. Visual Aids:

- Use diagrams to show how the iterator progresses through the collection.
- Provide real-world analogies, such as sorting toys or counting steps.

**This approach helps students understand the concept of custom iterators, offering hands-on experience with creating and using iterators in a fun and engaging way.**

## Generator functions

### Teaching Generators: Understanding Generator Functions

**Objective: Introduce young learners to generator functions using simple explanations and interactive examples.**

# 1. Introduction to Generators:

- **Definition:** Generator functions are a type of iterator that allows you to iterate through a sequence of values, producing one value at a time using the yield keyword. They are efficient and convenient for generating sequences on the fly.
- **Analogy:** "Think of a generator function as a magic hat that gives you one item at a time whenever you need it, without having to hold all items in memory."

# 2. Creating a Generator Function:

- **Steps:**

1. **Define a Function:** Create a function that will act as the generator.
2. **Use yield:** Instead of return, use yield to produce values one at a time.
3. **Iterate Through Values:** Use a loop to get each value from the generator.

- **Example Code:**

```
# Define the generator function
    def magic_hat():
    yield "Teddy Bear"
    yield "Ball"
    yield "Toy Car"

# Create a generator object
```

```
hat = magic_hat()
```

```
# Iterate through the values
for toy in hat:
print(toy)
```

**Explanation:**

- magic_hat is our generator function.
- yield provides each item one by one.
- hat is the generator object created from magic_hat.
- for toy in hat retrieves and prints each value.

## 3. Benefits of Generators:

- **Memory Efficiency:**
- Generators are memory-efficient because they generate values on-the-fly, instead of storing them all in memory.
- **Lazy Evaluation:**
- They produce values only when needed, making them ideal for handling large datasets.

## 4. Interactive Examples:

- **Example 1:** Create a generator function that yields a sequence of numbers or characters.
- **Example 2:** Use a generator to produce a sequence of simple shapes or objects.

## 5. Hands-On Activities:

- **Activity 1:** Have students create their own generator function that yields their favorite animals or toys.
- **Activity 2:** Implement a generator that counts down from a number and use it to demonstrate the concept.

## 6. Visual Aids:

- Use diagrams to illustrate how a generator produces values one at a time.
- Provide analogies such as a magician pulling items from a hat to visualize the concept.

**This approach helps students grasp the concept of generator functions by offering practical experience with creating and using generators in a fun and engaging manner.**

## yield statement

Teaching yield Statement: Understanding Generator Functions

**Objective: Introduce students to the yield statement in generator functions, with a focus on simplicity and practical examples.**

# 1. Introduction to yield:

- **Definition:** The yield statement is used in generator functions to produce a series of values over time, allowing the function to be paused and resumed. It is an efficient way to iterate through sequences without holding all values in memory at once.
- **Analogy:** "Think of yield as a magic word that tells the function to hand out one item at a time, and then pause until you're ready for the next item."

# 2. Using the yield Statement:

- **Steps:**

1. **Define a Generator Function:** Create a function that uses yield to produce values.
2. **Use yield to Return Values:** Each yield provides a value and pauses the function.
3. **Resume with __next__:** The function resumes from where it left off when requested.

- **Example Code:**

```
# Define the generator function with yield
def magic_hat():
yield "Teddy Bear" # Yield the first item
yield "Ball" # Yield the second item
yield "Toy Car" # Yield the third item

# Create a generator object
```

132

```
hat = magic_hat()
```

```
# Iterate through the values
for toy in hat:
print(toy)
```

**Explanation:**

- magic_hat is our generator function.
- Each yield provides a value from the sequence.
- hat is the generator object created from magic_hat.
- for toy in hat iterates through the values, one by one.

## 3. Benefits of Using yield:

- **Memory Efficiency:**
- Generators using yield are memory-efficient as they produce values one at a time.
- **Lazy Evaluation:**
- Values are generated only when needed, making it suitable for large datasets.

## 4. Interactive Examples:

- **Example 1:** Create a generator function that yields a sequence of simple numbers or characters.
- **Example 2:** Use yield to produce a series of objects or names, demonstrating the concept of pausing and resuming.

## 5. Hands-On Activities:

- **Activity 1:** Have students create a generator function that yields their favorite animals or toys, using yield to return each one.
- **Activity 2:** Implement a generator that counts up or down, showcasing how yield controls the flow of values.

## 6. Visual Aids:

- Use diagrams to show how yield produces and pauses values.
- Provide real-world analogies, such as a magician pulling items from a hat, to illustrate the concept.

**This approach helps students understand the yield statement by offering hands-on experience with creating and using generators in a fun and engaging manner.**

# Chapter 14 Decorators

Function decorators

Teaching Function Decorators: Understanding
Function Wrapping

Objective: Introduce students to function decorators by explaining how they wrap functions to
add additional behavior. Use simple examples
and analogies to illustrate the concept.

1. Introduction to Function Decorators:

- **Definition:** Function decorators are a way to modify or
  extend the behavior of functions without changing their
  actual code. They "decorate" or "wrap" around the original
  function to add extra functionality.
- **Analogy:** "Think of a decorator as adding extra decorations to a cake. The cake (function) remains the same, but

the decorations (decorator) add special touches."

## 2. Creating and Using a Function Decorator:

- **Steps:**

1. **Define the Decorator:**

- Create a function that takes another function as an argument and returns a new function with added behavior.

1. **Apply the Decorator:**

- Use the @decorator_name syntax to apply the decorator to the function you want to modify.
- **Example Code:**

python
```
Copy code
# Define the decorator function
def sparkle_decorator(func):
def wrapper():
print("✦✦✦ Sparkling before the magic! ✦✦✦")
func()
print("✦✦✦ Sparkling after the magic! ✦✦✦")
return wrapper
```

```
# Define the original function
def magic_hat():
print("Here's a toy!")
```

```python
# Apply the decorator to the function
@sparkle_decorator
def magic_hat():
    print("Here's a toy!")
```

```python
# Call the decorated function
magic_hat()
```

**Explanation:**

- sparkle_decorator is the decorator function that adds extra behavior.
- magic_hat is the original function.
- The decorator is applied using the @sparkle_decorator syntax, which modifies the magic_hat function to include the extra behavior defined in the decorator.

## 3. Benefits of Using Decorators:

- **Code Reusability:**
- Decorators allow you to reuse code for adding the same behavior to multiple functions.
- **Separation of Concerns:**
- They help separate the additional behavior from the core functionality of the function.

## 4. Interactive Examples:

- **Example 1:** Create a decorator that adds logging or timing functionality to a function.
- **Example 2:** Implement a decorator that modifies the output of a function, such as adding special characters

or formatting.

## 5. Hands-On Activities:

- **Activity 1:** Have students create their own decorators to add different features (e.g., logging messages or special prints) to their functions.
- **Activity 2:** Use a real-world analogy, such as decorating a birthday cake, to help students visualize how decorators add extra features.

## 6. Visual Aids:

- Use diagrams to show how decorators wrap around functions and add extra behavior.
- Provide analogies and simple examples to illustrate the concept of function wrapping.

**This approach helps students grasp the concept of function decorators by providing hands-on experience and practical examples, making it easier to understand and apply the concept.**

## Class decorators

## Introduction to Class Decorators

**Objective: Explain what class decorators are and how they enhance classes by adding additional features or behaviors.**

- **Definition:**
- Class decorators are functions that modify or extend the behavior of classes. They allow you to add new features or change the behavior of entire classes.
- **Analogy:**
- Think of class decorators as adding special decorations to a whole classroom (class) to enhance its functionality.

## Creating and Using Class Decorators

- **Creating a Class Decorator:**
- A class decorator is a function that takes a class as an argument and returns a new class with additional features or modifications.
- **Example Code:**

```
def sparkle_class_decorator(cls):
    class WrappedClass(cls):
    def new_method(self):
    print("✧✧✧ Extra sparkle added! ✧✧✧")
```

```
return WrappedClass
```

- **Applying the Class Decorator:**
- Use the @decorator_name syntax to apply the decorator

to a class.
- **Example Code:**

```
@sparkle_class_decorator
  class MagicClass:
  def original_method(self):
  print("This is the original magic!")

magic_object = MagicClass()
  magic_object.original_method()
  magic_object.new_method()
```

- **Benefits of Class Decorators:**
- **Enhanced Functionality:**
- Class decorators can add new methods or change the behavior of existing methods in a class.
- **Code Organization:**
- They help keep class definitions clean and separate from additional features.
- **Interactive Examples:**
- Create class decorators that add new methods or modify existing ones in a class.
- Demonstrate how decorators can be used to enhance class functionality.
- **Hands-On Activities:**
- Students create their own class decorators to add features to their classes.
- Implement class decorators to show practical applications.

**This approach helps students understand how to use class decorators to enhance classes, making their code more**

**flexible and feature-rich.**

# 19

# Chapter 15 Regular Expressions

## Basic pattern matching

### Introduction to Basic Pattern Matching

bjective: Explain what basic pattern matching is and how to use simple patterns to find specific text or numbers.

- **Definition:**
- Basic pattern matching involves using special symbols to search for patterns in text. It helps us find specific words or numbers by defining a search pattern.
- **Analogy:**
- Think of it as using a search tool to look for specific items in a large collection. Patterns guide the search tool to find what we're looking for.

## Using Basic Pattern Matching

- **Creating a Pattern:**
- Use special symbols to define the pattern you want to search for.
- **Example Code:**

```
import re

# Create a pattern to find a specific word
pattern = "cat"
text = "The cat is on the mat."

# Search for the pattern in the text
result = re.search(pattern, text)
if result:
print("✧ Found the word 'cat'! ✧")
else:
print("No 'cat' found.")
```

- **Symbols Used in Patterns:**
- . (dot): Represents any character.
- * (star): Represents zero or more occurrences of the previous character.
- ^ (caret): Matches the start of a string.
- $ (dollar sign): Matches the end of a string.
- **Benefits of Basic Pattern Matching:**
- **Efficient Searching:**
- Quickly locate specific words or numbers in large texts.
- **Flexible Patterns:**
- Customize patterns to match different types of text or

numbers.
- **Interactive Examples:**
- Create patterns to find different words or numbers in various texts.
- Show how patterns can be adjusted to search for different criteria.
- **Hands-On Activities:**
- Students create their own patterns to search for words or numbers in provided texts.
- Implement practical exercises to reinforce the concept.

**This approach ensures that students understand the basics of pattern matching and how to use patterns to search for specific items in text in a fun and engaging way.**

## Search and replace

### Introduction to Search and Replace

**Objective: Explain what search and replace is and how to use regular expressions to find and replace specific text or numbers.**

- **Definition:**
- Search and replace involves using a pattern to find specific text and then replacing it with different text. This is useful for quickly modifying large texts.
- **Analogy:**
- Think of it as using a magic wand to instantly transform

specific items in a large collection. The pattern guides the transformation.

## Using Search and Replace

- **Creating a Pattern:**
- Use regular expressions to define the pattern you want to search for and specify the replacement text.
- **Example Code:**

```
import re

# Define the pattern and replacement
pattern = "cat"
replacement = "dog"
text = "The cat is on the mat."

# Perform search and replace
new_text = re.sub(pattern, replacement, text)
print(new_text) # Output: The dog is on the mat.
```

- **Benefits of Search and Replace:**
- **Efficient Text Modification:**
- Quickly change specific words or numbers in large texts.
- **Flexible Patterns:**
- Customize patterns to match and replace different types of text.
- **Interactive Examples:**
- Create patterns to find and replace different words or numbers in various texts.
- Show how patterns can be adjusted to perform different

types of replacements.
- **Hands-On Activities:**
- Students create their own patterns to search for and replace words or numbers in provided texts.
- Implement practical exercises to reinforce the concept.

**This approach ensures that students understand the basics of search and replace and how to use patterns to modify text in a fun and engaging way.**

## Grouping and capturing

### Introduction to Grouping and Capturing

**Objective: Explain what grouping and capturing is and how to use regular expressions to find and capture specific groups of text or numbers.**

- **Definition:**
- Grouping and capturing involves using parentheses in regular expressions to create groups that can be accessed later. This is useful for extracting specific parts of text.
- **Analogy:**
- Think of it as using a net to catch specific groups of items in a large collection. The groups can then be used for various purposes.

## Using Grouping and Capturing

- **Creating a Group:**
- Use parentheses () in regular expressions to define the groups you want to capture.
- **Example Code:**

```
import re

# Define the pattern to find a greeting followed by a name
pattern = r"(hello) (\w+)"
text = "hello John, hello Jane"

# Perform the search
result = re.search(pattern, text)
if result:
print(f"✧ Found: {result.group(0)}") # The whole match
print(f"✧ Greeting: {result.group(1)}") # The first group
(hello)
print(f"✧ Name: {result.group(2)}") # The second group (the
name)
else:
print("No match found.")
```

- **Benefits of Grouping and Capturing:**
- **Efficient Text Extraction:**
- Quickly capture and use specific parts of text.
- **Flexible Grouping:**
- Customize groups to capture different parts of text.
- **Interactive Examples:**
- Create patterns to find and capture different groups of

words or numbers in various texts.
- Show how groups can be used to perform different types of text manipulation.
- **Hands-On Activities:**
- Students create their own patterns to capture groups of words or numbers in provided texts.
- Implement practical exercises to reinforce the concept.

**This approach ensures that students understand the basics of grouping and capturing and how to use patterns to extract specific parts of text in a fun and engaging way.**

# 20

# Chapter 16 Concurrency

## Multithreading

### Introduction to Multithreading

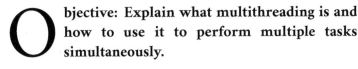 bjective: Explain what multithreading is and how to use it to perform multiple tasks simultaneously.

- **Definition:**
- Multithreading involves creating multiple threads, which are like smaller units of a program, to run different tasks concurrently. This is useful for improving the efficiency of programs.
- **Analogy:**
- Think of it as having multiple magical helpers (threads) that can perform different tasks at the same time, speeding up the overall process.

## Using Multithreading

- **Creating Threads:**
- Use the threading library to create and manage threads.
- **Example Code:**

```python
import threading

# Define a task for the thread
def magic_task(name):
    for i in range(3):
        print(f"{name} is doing a magical task {i}")

# Create threads
thread1 = threading.Thread(target=magic_task, args=("Wand 1",))
thread2 = threading.Thread(target=magic_task, args=("Wand 2",))
thread3 = threading.Thread(target=magic_task, args=("Wand 3",))

# Start the threads
thread1.start()
thread2.start()
thread3.start()

# Wait for all threads to finish
thread1.join()
thread2.join()
thread3.join()
```

- **Benefits of Multithreading:**
- **Efficient Task Management:**
- Perform multiple tasks simultaneously, improving program efficiency.
- **Flexible Task Execution:**
- Customize threads to perform different types of tasks.
- **Interactive Examples:**
- Create threads to perform different tasks, demonstrating how multiple tasks can be executed concurrently.
- Show how threads can be managed and synchronized to ensure proper execution.
- **Hands-On Activities:**
- Students create their own threads to perform various tasks, reinforcing the concept of multithreading.
- Implement practical exercises to demonstrate the benefits of multithreading.

**This approach ensures that students understand the basics of multithreading and how to use it to perform multiple tasks concurrently in a fun and engaging way.**

## Multiprocessing

### Introduction to Multiprocessing

**Objective: Explain what multiprocessing is and how to use it to perform large tasks simultaneously.**

- **Definition:**

- Multiprocessing involves creating multiple processes, which are like separate programs, to run different tasks concurrently. This is useful for improving the efficiency of programs, especially for tasks that require a lot of computational power.
- **Analogy:**
- Think of it as having multiple superheroes (processes) that can perform different big tasks at the same time, speeding up the overall process.

## Using Multiprocessing

- **Creating Processes:**
- Use the multiprocessing library to create and manage processes.
- **Example Code:**

```
import multiprocessing

# Define a task for the process
  def magic_task(name):
  for i in range(3):
  print(f"{name} is doing a super magical task {i}")


# Create processes
  process1 = multiprocessing.Process(target=magic_task,
args=("Superhero 1",))
  process2 = multiprocessing.Process(target=magic_task,
args=("Superhero 2",))
  process3 = multiprocessing.Process(target=magic_task,
args=("Superhero 3",))
```

```
# Start the processes
process1.start()
process2.start()
process3.start()

# Wait for all processes to finish
process1.join()
process2.join()
process3.join()
```

- **Benefits of Multiprocessing:**
- **Efficient Task Management:**
- Perform large tasks simultaneously, improving program efficiency.
- **Flexible Task Execution:**
- Customize processes to perform different types of large tasks.
- **Interactive Examples:**
- Create processes to perform different large tasks, demonstrating how multiple tasks can be executed concurrently.
- Show how processes can be managed and synchronized to ensure proper execution.
- **Hands-On Activities:**
- Students create their own processes to perform various large tasks, reinforcing the concept of multiprocessing.
- Implement practical exercises to demonstrate the benefits of multiprocessing.

**This approach ensures that students understand the basics of multiprocessing and how to use it to perform large tasks concurrently in a fun and engaging way.**

153

## Asyncio (asynchronous programming)

### Introduction to Asyncio

**Objective: Explain what asyncio is and how to use it to perform tasks without waiting.**

- **Definition:**
- Asyncio is a Python library that provides tools for writing asynchronous programs. It allows for concurrent code execution without using traditional multi-threading or multiprocessing.
- **Analogy:**
- Think of it as a wizard who can handle multiple spells at the same time by quickly switching between them, allowing tasks to progress without waiting for others to finish.

### Using Asyncio

- **Creating Asynchronous Tasks:**
- Use the asyncio library to create and manage asynchronous tasks.
- **Example Code:**

```
import asyncio

# Define an asynchronous task
    async def magic_task(name):
    for i in range(3):
    print(f"{name} is doing a speedy magical task {i}")
    await asyncio.sleep(1) # Simulate a small wait without
```

stopping other tasks

```python
# Create an event loop to run our tasks
async def main():
    task1 = asyncio.create_task(magic_task("Wizard 1"))
    task2 = asyncio.create_task(magic_task("Wizard 2"))
    task3 = asyncio.create_task(magic_task("Wizard 3"))

# Wait for all tasks to finish
    await task1
    await task2
    await task3

# Run the event loop
asyncio.run(main())
```

- **Benefits of Asyncio:**
- **Efficient Task Management:**
- Perform multiple tasks without waiting, improving program efficiency.
- **Flexible Task Execution:**
- Customize asynchronous tasks to perform different types of operations.
- **Interactive Examples:**
- Create asynchronous tasks to perform different operations, demonstrating how tasks can progress without waiting.
- Show how tasks can be managed and synchronized to ensure proper execution.
- **Hands-On Activities:**
- Students create their own asynchronous tasks to perform

various operations, reinforcing the concept of asyncio.
- Implement practical exercises to demonstrate the benefits of asynchronous programming.

**This approach ensures that students understand the basics of asyncio and how to use it to perform tasks without waiting in a fun and engaging way.**


Advanced

# 21

# Chapter 17 Advanced OOP Concepts

## Meta-classes

### Introduction to Meta-classes

Objective: **Explain what meta-classes are and how to use them to define the rules for creating other classes.**

- **Definition:**
- Meta-classes are classes of classes, defining how classes behave. They allow for customizing class creation and modifying class attributes and methods.
- **Analogy:**
- Think of meta-classes as master builders who create blueprints for making different kinds of castles (classes).

## Using Meta-classes

- **Creating Meta-classes:**
- Use the type class to define meta-classes that control the creation of other classes.
- **Example Code:**

```
# Define a meta-class
class MasterBuilder(type):
def __new__(cls, name, bases, dct):
print(f"Creating a new class called {name}")
return super().__new__(cls, name, bases, dct)
```

```
# Define a class using the meta-class
class Castle(metaclass=MasterBuilder):
def __init__(self, name):
self.name = name
```

```
# Create an instance of the class
my_castle = Castle("Awesome Castle")
print(my_castle.name)
```

- **Benefits of Meta-classes:**
- **Customizing Class Creation:**
- Control how classes are created and modify class attributes and methods.
- **Flexible Class Design:**
- Create blueprints for making different kinds of classes, allowing for efficient class creation.
- **Interactive Examples:**
- Create meta-classes to define rules for creating different

types of classes, demonstrating how meta-classes control class behavior.

- Show how meta-classes can modify class attributes and methods during class creation.
- **Hands-On Activities:**
- Students create their own meta-classes to define rules for creating various classes, reinforcing the concept of meta-classes.
- Implement practical exercises to demonstrate the benefits of using meta-classes.

**This approach ensures that students understand the basics of meta-classes and how to use them to define the rules for creating other classes in a fun and engaging way.**

## Class decorators

### Introduction to Class Decorators

**Objective: Explain what class decorators are and how to use them to add features or modify classes.**

- **Definition:**
- Class decorators are functions that add extra features or change the behavior of classes. They are applied to classes using the @ symbol followed by the decorator function name.
- **Analogy:**

- Think of class decorators as magical stickers that enhance classes with new features or change how they work.

## Using Class Decorators

- **Creating Class Decorators:**
- Define a function that takes a class as an argument, modifies it, and returns the modified class.
- **Example Code:**

```
# Define a class decorator
  def magic_sticker(cls):
  cls.magic_power = "Zooms Super Fast!"
  return cls
```

```
# Define a class using the decorator
  @magic_sticker
  class ToyCar:
  def __init__(self, name):
  self.name = name
```

```
def drive(self):
  print(f"{self.name} is driving!")
```

```
# Create an instance of the class
  my_car = ToyCar("Speedy")
  print(my_car.magic_power) # Output: Zooms Super Fast!
```

- **Benefits of Class Decorators:**
- **Adding Features:**
- Add new attributes or methods to classes.

- **Modifying Behavior:**
- Change how classes behave or add special abilities.
- **Interactive Examples:**
- Create class decorators to add features to different classes, demonstrating how decorators can enhance class behavior.
- Show how decorators can be used to modify existing classes and add new capabilities.
- **Hands-On Activities:**
- Students create their own class decorators to add new features or modify classes, reinforcing the concept of class decorators.
- Implement practical exercises to demonstrate the benefits of using class decorators.

**This approach ensures that students understand the basics of class decorators and how to use them to enhance or modify classes in a fun and engaging way.**

## Abstract base classes

### Introduction to Abstract Base Classes

**Objective: Explain what abstract base classes are and how to use them to define rules for other classes.**

- **Definition:**
- Abstract Base Classes (ABCs) are classes that define methods that other classes must implement. They use the ABC module and the abstractmethod decorator to define

abstract methods.
- **Analogy:**
- Think of ABCs as club leaders who set rules for all club members to follow, ensuring that everyone behaves in a certain way.

## Using Abstract Base Classes

- **Creating Abstract Base Classes:**
- Use the ABC module and abstractmethod decorator to define abstract methods that must be implemented by subclasses.
- **Example Code:**

```python
from abc import ABC, abstractmethod

# Define an abstract base class
class ClubLeader(ABC):
    @abstractmethod
    def say_hello(self):
        pass

# Define a subclass that implements the abstract method
class ClubMember(ClubLeader):
    def say_hello(self):
        print("Hello, I'm a club member!")

# Create an instance of the subclass
member = ClubMember()
member.say_hello() # Output: Hello, I'm a club member!
```

- **Benefits of Abstract Base Classes:**
- **Setting Rules:**
- Define methods that must be implemented by subclasses, ensuring consistent behavior across different classes.
- **Ensuring Consistency:**
- Provide a blueprint for subclasses, making sure they all have certain methods.
- **Interactive Examples:**
- Create ABCs to define rules for different classes, demonstrating how abstract methods enforce consistent behavior.
- Show how subclasses must implement abstract methods, ensuring they follow the rules set by the ABC.
- **Hands-On Activities:**
- Students create their own ABCs to set rules for different classes, reinforcing the concept of abstract base classes.
- Implement practical exercises to demonstrate the benefits of using ABCs to ensure consistency across classes.

**This approach ensures that students understand the basics of abstract base classes and how to use them to define rules for other classes in a fun and engaging way.**

# 22

# Chapter 18 Data Structures and Algorithms

## Arrays and linked lists

### Introduction to Arrays and Linked Lists

**O**bjective: **Explain what arrays and linked lists are and how to use them to store and organize items.**

- **Definition:**
- **Arrays:** Arrays are data structures that store items in a specific order, like a toy box with compartments.
- **Linked Lists:** Linked lists are data structures that store items in a chain of nodes, like a toy train with connected cars.

## Using Arrays and Linked Lists

- **Arrays:**
- Use arrays to store and organize items in a specific order.
- **Example Code:**

```
# Define an array (toy box)
toy_box = ["car", "doll", "ball", "robot"]
```

```
# Access an item in the array
favorite_toy = toy_box[2]
print(f"My favorite toy is: {favorite_toy}") # Output: My favorite toy is: ball
```

- **Linked Lists:**
- Use linked lists to create a flexible chain of items that can grow or shrink easily.
- **Example Code:**

```
# Define a node (train car)
class TrainCar:
def __init__(self, toy):
self.toy = toy
self.next = None
```

```
# Create nodes (train cars)
car1 = TrainCar("car")
car2 = TrainCar("doll")
car3 = TrainCar("ball")
```

```
# Connect the nodes (link the train cars)
```

```
car1.next = car2
car2.next = car3

# Traverse the linked list (train)
current_car = car1
while current_car is not None:
print(f"This train car has a: {current_car.toy}")
current_car = current_car.next
# Output:
# This train car has a: car
# This train car has a: doll
# This train car has a: ball
```

- **Interactive Examples:**
- Create arrays and linked lists to demonstrate how to store and organize items in different ways.
- Show how arrays provide easy access to items and how linked lists offer flexibility in adding or removing items.
- **Hands-On Activities:**
- Students create their own arrays and linked lists to store and organize their favorite toys, reinforcing the concepts of arrays and linked lists.
- Implement practical exercises to demonstrate the benefits of using arrays and linked lists in different scenarios.

**This approach ensures that students understand the basics of arrays and linked lists and how to use them to store and organize items in a fun and engaging way.**

## Stacks and queues

### Introduction to Stacks and Queues

**Objective: Explain what stacks and queues are and how to use them to store and organize items in specific orders.**

- **Definition:**
- **Stacks:** Stacks are data structures that store items in a Last-In-First-Out (LIFO) order, like a pile of pancakes.
- **Queues:** Queues are data structures that store items in a First-In-First-Out (FIFO) order, like a line of toys.

### Using Stacks and Queues

- **Stacks:**
- Use stacks to keep track of things in a LIFO order.
- **Example Code:**

```
# Define a stack (pancake pile)
pancake_stack = []
```

```
# Add items to the stack
pancake_stack.append("pancake1")
pancake_stack.append("pancake2")
pancake_stack.append("pancake3")
```

```
print(f"Pancakes in stack: {pancake_stack}") # Output: Pancakes in stack: ['pancake1', 'pancake2', 'pancake3']
```

```
# Remove an item from the stack
```

```
eaten_pancake = pancake_stack.pop()
print(f"Ate {eaten_pancake}") # Output: Ate pancake3
print(f"Pancakes left in stack: {pancake_stack}") # Output:
Pancakes left in stack: ['pancake1', 'pancake2']
```

- **Queues:**
- Use queues to keep track of things in a FIFO order.
- **Example Code:**

```
from collections import deque

# Define a queue (toy line)
   toy_queue = deque()

# Add items to the queue
   toy_queue.append("toy1")
   toy_queue.append("toy2")
   toy_queue.append("toy3")

print(f"Toys in queue: {toy_queue}") # Output: Toys in queue:
deque(['toy1', 'toy2', 'toy3'])

# Remove an item from the queue
   first_toy = toy_queue.popleft()
   print(f"Played with {first_toy}") # Output: Played with toy1
   print(f"Toys left in queue: {toy_queue}") # Output: Toys left
in queue: deque(['toy2', 'toy3'])
```

- **Interactive Examples:**
- Create stacks and queues to demonstrate how to store and organize items in different orders.

- Show how stacks provide a LIFO order and queues offer a FIFO order.
- **Hands-On Activities:**
- Students create their own stacks and queues to store and organize their favorite toys, reinforcing the concepts of stacks and queues.
- Implement practical exercises to demonstrate the benefits of using stacks and queues in different scenarios.

**This approach ensures that students understand the basics of stacks and queues and how to use them to store and organize items in a fun and engaging way.**

# Trees (binary trees, binary search trees, AVL trees)

## Introduction to Trees

**Objective: Explain what binary trees, binary search trees, and AVL trees are and how they can be used to organize data.**

- **Definitions:**
- **Binary Trees:** Trees with nodes that have up to two children.
- **Binary Search Trees (BSTs):** Binary trees where each node follows the rule: left child < parent < right child.
- **AVL Trees:** Self-balancing binary search trees.

## Using Trees

- **Binary Trees:**
- Use to organize data hierarchically.
- **Example Code:**

```
class TreeNode:
    def __init__(self, value):
    self.value = value
    self.left = None
    self.right = None
```

```
# Create the root of the tree
    root = TreeNode("root")
```

```
# Add children to the root
    root.left = TreeNode("left_child")
    root.right = TreeNode("right_child")
```

```
print(f"Root: {root.value}") # Output: Root: root
    print(f"Left child: {root.left.value}") # Output: Left child:
left_child
    print(f"Right child: {root.right.value}") # Output: Right child:
right_child
```

- **Binary Search Trees (BSTs):**
- Use to quickly find, add, and remove items.
- **Example Code:**

```
class TreeNode:
    def __init__(self, value):
```

```python
        self.value = value
        self.left = None
        self.right = None

class BinarySearchTree:
    def __init__(self):
        self.root = None

def insert(self, value):
    if not self.root:
        self.root = TreeNode(value)
    else:
        self._insert_recursive(self.root, value)

def _insert_recursive(self, node, value):
    if value < node.value:
        if node.left is None:
        node.left = TreeNode(value)
        else:
        self._insert_recursive(node.left, value)
        else:
        if node.right is None:
        node.right = TreeNode(value)
        else:
        self._insert_recursive(node.right, value)

# Create the BST and add values
    bst = BinarySearchTree()
    bst.insert(5)
    bst.insert(3)
    bst.insert(7)
```

171

```
print(f"Root: {bst.root.value}") # Output: Root: 5
    print(f"Left child: {bst.root.left.value}") # Output: Left child:
3
    print(f"Right child: {bst.root.right.value}") # Output: Right
child: 7
```

## AVL Trees:

- Use to keep data balanced and accessible.
- **Example Code:**

```
class TreeNode:
    def __init__(self, value):
    self.value = value
    self.left = None
    self.right = None
    self.height = 1


class AVLTree:
    def __init__(self):
    self.root = None


def insert(self, root, value):
    if not root:
    return TreeNode(value)
    elif value < root.value:
    root.left = self.insert(root.left, value)
    else:
    root.right = self.insert(root.right, value)

root.height = 1 + max(self.get_height(root.left), self.get_height(root.right))
```

```python
    balance = self.get_balance(root)

if balance > 1 and value < root.left.value:
    return self.right_rotate(root)
    if balance < -1 and value > root.right.value:
    return self.left_rotate(root)
    if balance > 1 and value > root.left.value:
    root.left = self.left_rotate(root.left)
    return self.right_rotate(root)
    if balance < -1 and value < root.right.value:
    root.right = self.right_rotate(root.right)
    return self.left_rotate(root)

return root

def left_rotate(self, z):
    y = z.right
    T2 = y.left
    y.left = z
    z.right = T2
    z.height = 1 + max(self.get_height(z.left), self.get_height(z.right))
    y.height = 1 + max(self.get_height(y.left), self.get_height(y.right))
    return y

def right_rotate(self, z):
    y = z.left
    T3 = y.right
    y.right = z
    z.left = T3
    z.height = 1 + max(self.get_height(z.left), self.get_height(z.right))
    y.height = 1 + max(self.get_height(y.left), self.get_height(y.right))
```

```
    return y

def get_height(self, root):
    if not root:
    return 0
    return root.height

def get_balance(self, root):
    if not root:
    return 0
    return self.get_height(root.left) - self.get_height(root.right)

# Create the AVL tree and add values
    avl = AVLTree()
    root = None
    values = [10, 20, 30, 40, 50, 25]
    for value in values:
    root = avl.insert(root, value)

print(f"Root: {root.value}") # Output: Root: 30
```

- **Interactive Examples:**
- Create trees with students to demonstrate hierarchical data organization.
- Show how BSTs offer efficient data lookup by comparing it to a simple search through a list.
- **Hands-On Activities:**
- Students create their own binary trees, BSTs, and AVL trees with toy examples.
- Implement practical exercises to reinforce the concept of trees and their use cases.

**This approach ensures that students grasp the basics of binary trees, binary search trees, and AVL trees in a fun and engaging way.**

## Graphs (BFS, DFS, Dijkstra's algorithm)

### Introduction to Graphs

**Objective: Explain what graphs are and how they can be used to represent various types of data. Introduce the concepts of BFS, DFS, and Dijkstra's algorithm with practical examples.**

- **Definitions:**
- **Graphs:** Data structures consisting of nodes (vertices) and edges.
- **BFS:** Algorithm for traversing or searching tree or graph data structures.
- **DFS:** Algorithm for traversing or searching tree or graph data structures.
- **Dijkstra's Algorithm:** Algorithm for finding the shortest paths between nodes in a graph.

### Using Graphs

- **BFS:**
- Use to explore nodes level by level.
- **Example Code:**

```
from collections import deque
```

```
def bfs(graph, start):
    visited = set()
    queue = deque([start])

while queue:
    node = queue.popleft()
    if node not in visited:
    print(node, end=" ") # Visit the node
    visited.add(node)
    queue.extend(graph[node])

graph = {
    'A': ['B', 'C'],
    'B': ['D', 'E'],
    'C': ['F', 'G'],
    'D': [],
    'E': [],
    'F': [],
    'G': []
    }

bfs(graph, 'A') # Output: A B C D E F G
```

- **DFS:**
- Use to explore nodes deeply before backtracking.
- **Example Code:**

```
def dfs(graph, start, visited=None):
    if visited is None:
    visited = set()
    visited.add(start)
```

```python
print(start, end=" ") # Visit the node

for neighbor in graph[start]:
    if neighbor not in visited:
        dfs(graph, neighbor, visited)

graph = {
    'A': ['B', 'C'],
    'B': ['D', 'E'],
    'C': ['F', 'G'],
    'D': [],
    'E': [],
    'F': [],
    'G': []
}

dfs(graph, 'A') # Output: A B D E C F G
```

- **Dijkstra's Algorithm:**
- Use to find the shortest path in weighted graphs.
- **Example Code:**

```python
import heapq

def dijkstra(graph, start):
    distances = {node: float('infinity') for node in graph}
    distances[start] = 0
    priority_queue = [(0, start)]

while priority_queue:
    current_distance, current_node = heapq.heappop(prior-
```

```
ity_queue)

if current_distance > distances[current_node]:
    continue

for neighbor, weight in graph[current_node]:
    distance = current_distance + weight

if distance < distances[neighbor]:
    distances[neighbor] = distance
    heapq.heappush(priority_queue, (distance, neighbor))

return distances

graph = {
    'A': [('B', 1), ('C', 4)],
    'B': [('A', 1), ('D', 2), ('E', 5)],
    'C': [('A', 4), ('F', 6)],
    'D': [('B', 2)],
    'E': [('B', 5)],
    'F': [('C', 6)]
}

print(dijkstra(graph, 'A')) # Output: {'A': 0, 'B': 1, 'C': 4, 'D': 3,
'E': 6, 'F': 10}
```

- **Interactive Examples:**
- Create small graph examples with students to demonstrate BFS, DFS, and Dijkstra's algorithm.
- **Hands-On Activities:**
- Students create their own graphs and apply BFS, DFS, and

Dijkstra's algorithm.

**This approach ensures that students grasp the basics of graphs, BFS, DFS, and Dijkstra's algorithm in a fun and engaging way.**

## Hash tables

### Introduction to Hash Tables

**Objective: Explain what hash tables are, how they work, and their advantages. Introduce the concept of hash functions and collision handling.**

- **Definitions:**
- **Hash Table:** A data structure that stores items using key-value pairs.
- **Key:** A unique identifier for an item.
- **Value:** The actual item stored in the hash table.
- **Hash Function:** A function that converts a key into an index for storage.
- **Collision:** When two keys produce the same index.

### Using Hash Tables

- **Storing and Finding Items:**
- **Example Code:**

```
hash_table = {}
```

```python
# Storing items
hash_table['toy_car'] = 'red car'
hash_table['doll'] = 'Barbie'
hash_table['lego'] = 'Lego set'

# Finding items
print(hash_table['toy_car']) # Output: red car
print(hash_table['doll']) # Output: Barbie
```

- **Hash Functions:**
- **Example Code:**

```python
def hash_function(key):
    return len(key) % 10 # A simple hash function

print(hash_function('apple')) # Output: 5
print(hash_function('banana')) # Output: 6
```

- **Handling Collisions (Chaining):**
- **Example Code:**

```python
hash_table = {}

# Storing items with collisions
def store_item(key, value):
    index = hash_function(key)
    if index not in hash_table:
        hash_table[index] = []
        hash_table[index].append((key, value))

store_item('apple', 1)
```

180

store_item('banana', 2)

print(hash_table) # Output: {5: [('apple', 1)], 6: [('banana', 2)]}

- **Interactive Examples:**
- Create small hash table examples with students to demonstrate storing, finding, and handling collisions.
- **Hands-On Activities:**
- Students create their own hash tables and practice storing and retrieving items.

**This approach ensures that students grasp the basics of hash tables, hash functions, and collision handling in a fun and engaging way.**

# Heaps

## Introduction to Heaps

**Objective: Explain what heaps are, how they work, and their uses. Introduce heap operations and their benefits.**

- **Definitions:**
- **Heap:** A special tree structure where the smallest (min-heap) or largest (max-heap) item is always at the top.
- **Min-Heap:** The smallest item is at the top.
- **Max-Heap:** The largest item is at the top.
- **Heap Operations:** Adding and removing items from the heap.

## Using Heaps

- **Building a Min-Heap:**
- **Example Code:**

```
min_heap = []

def add_to_heap(heap, item):
  heap.append(item)
  index = len(heap) - 1
  while index > 0:
  parent_index = (index - 1) // 2
  if heap[index] < heap[parent_index]:
  heap[index], heap[parent_index] = heap[parent_index], heap[index]
  index = parent_index
  else:
  break

add_to_heap(min_heap, 3)
  add_to_heap(min_heap, 1)
  add_to_heap(min_heap, 6)
  add_to_heap(min_heap, 5)
  add_to_heap(min_heap, 9)
  add_to_heap(min_heap, 8)

print(min_heap) # Output: [1, 3, 6, 5, 9, 8]
```

- **Heap Operations (Using heapq):**
- **Example Code:**

```python
import heapq

numbers = [5, 1, 9, 3, 7]

# Convert list to min-heap
  heapq.heapify(numbers)
  print(numbers) # Output: [1, 3, 9, 5, 7]

# Add item to heap
  heapq.heappush(numbers, 2)
  print(numbers) # Output: [1, 2, 9, 5, 7, 3]

# Remove item from heap
  smallest = heapq.heappop(numbers)
  print(smallest) # Output: 1
  print(numbers) # Output: [2, 3, 9, 5, 7]
```

- **Interactive Examples:**
- Create small heap examples with students to demonstrate adding and removing items.
- **Hands-On Activities:**
- Students build their own heaps and practice heap operations.

**This approach ensures that students understand heaps, their operations, and uses in a fun and engaging way.**

# Sorting algorithms (quick sort, merge sort, bubble sort, insertion sort)

## Introduction to Sorting Algorithms

**Objective: Explain different sorting algorithms, how they work, and their real-life analogies. Provide fun activities and example codes to help young learners grasp the concepts.**

## 1. Bubble Sort

- **How It Works:**
- Compare two adjacent items.
- Swap them if they're in the wrong order.
- Continue until the entire list is sorted.
- **Example Code:**

```
def bubble_sort(items):
    n = len(items)
    for i in range(n):
    for j in range(0, n-i-1):
    if items[j] > items[j+1]:
    items[j], items[j+1] = items[j+1], items[j]

numbers = [5, 2, 9, 1, 5, 6]
    bubble_sort(numbers)
    print(numbers) # Output: [1, 2, 5, 5, 6, 9]
```

## 2. Insertion Sort

- **How It Works:**
- Start with the first item.
- Take the next item and insert it into its correct position.
- Repeat until the entire list is sorted.
- **Example Code:**

```
def insertion_sort(items):
    for i in range(1, len(items)):
    key = items[i]
    j = i - 1
    while j >= 0 and key < items[j]:
    items[j + 1] = items[j]
    j -= 1
    items[j + 1] = key

numbers = [12, 11, 13, 5, 6]
    insertion_sort(numbers)
    print(numbers) # Output: [5, 6, 11, 12, 13]
```

## 3. Merge Sort

- **How It Works:**
- Divide the list into two halves.
- Recursively sort each half.
- Merge the sorted halves back together.
- **Example Code:**

```
def merge_sort(items):
    if len(items) > 1:
```

```
    mid = len(items) // 2
    left_half = items[:mid]
    right_half = items[mid:]

merge_sort(left_half)
    merge_sort(right_half)

i = j = k = 0

while i < len(left_half) and j < len(right_half):
    if left_half[i] < right_half[j]:
    items[k] = left_half[i]
    i += 1
    else:
    items[k] = right_half[j]
    j += 1
    k += 1

while i < len(left_half):
    items[k] = left_half[i]
    i += 1
    k += 1

while j < len(right_half):
    items[k] = right_half[j]
    j += 1
    k += 1

numbers = [38, 27, 43, 3, 9, 82, 10]
    merge_sort(numbers)
    print(numbers) # Output: [3, 9, 10, 27, 38, 43, 82]
```

## 4. Quick Sort

- **How It Works:**
- Pick a pivot item.
- Partition the list so that items smaller than the pivot are on the left, and items larger are on the right.
- Recursively apply the same logic to the left and right parts.
- **Example Code:**

```
def quick_sort(items):
    if len(items) <= 1:
    return items
    else:
    pivot = items[0]
    less_than_pivot = [x for x in items[1:] if x <= pivot]
    greater_than_pivot = [x for x in items[1:] if x > pivot]
    return quick_sort(less_than_pivot) + [pivot] + quick_sort(greater_than_pivot)

numbers = [10, 7, 8, 9, 1, 5]
    sorted_numbers = quick_sort(numbers)
    print(sorted_numbers) # Output: [1, 5, 7, 8, 9, 10]
```

**This approach ensures that students understand various sorting algorithms, their working principles, and uses in a fun and engaging way.**

# Searching algorithms (linear search, binary search)

## Introduction to Searching Algorithms

**Objective: Explain different searching algorithms, how they work, and their real-life analogies. Provide fun activities and example codes to help young learners grasp the concepts.**

## 1. Linear Search

- **How It Works:**
- Start at the first item.
- Check each item until you find the target.
- Return the index of the target or -1 if not found.

- **Example Code:**

```
def linear_search(items, target):
    for i in range(len(items)):
    if items[i] == target:
    return i
    return -1

toys = ["car", "doll", "ball", "puzzle"]
    index = linear_search(toys, "ball")
    print(index) # Output: 2
```

## 2. Binary Search

- **How It Works:**
- Start in the middle of the list.
- Compare the middle item with the target.
- If the middle item is the target, return the index.
- If the middle item is less than the target, search the right half.
- If the middle item is greater than the target, search the left half.
- Repeat until the target is found or the search area is empty.
- **Example Code:**

```
def binary_search(items, target):
    left, right = 0, len(items) - 1
    while left <= right:
    mid = (left + right) // 2
    if items[mid] == target:
    return mid
    elif items[mid] < target:
    left = mid + 1
    else:
    right = mid - 1
    return -1
```

```
numbers = [1, 3, 5, 7, 9, 11]
    index = binary_search(numbers, 7)
    print(index) # Output: 3
```

**This approach ensures that students understand various searching algorithms, their working principles, and uses in a fun and engaging way.**

# Dynamic programming (Knapsack problem, Fibonacci sequence)

## Introduction to Dynamic Programming

**Objective: Explain the concept of dynamic programming and how it helps in solving complex problems efficiently by remembering previously computed results. Use fun analogies and simple examples to engage young learners.**

## 1. Knapsack Problem

- **How It Works:**
- Create a table dp where dp[i][w] represents the maximum value achievable with the first i items and a weight limit w.
- For each item, decide whether to include it based on its weight and value.
- **Example Code:**

```
def knapsack(weights, values, capacity):
  n = len(weights)
  dp = [[0] * (capacity + 1) for _ in range(n + 1)]

for i in range(1, n + 1):
  for w in range(capacity + 1):
    if weights[i-1] <= w:
    dp[i][w] = max(dp[i-1][w], dp[i-1][w-weights[i-1]] + values[i-1])
    else:
```

```
dp[i][w] = dp[i-1][w]

return dp[n][capacity]

weights = [1, 2, 3]
  values = [10, 20, 30]
  capacity = 5
  max_value = knapsack(weights, values, capacity)
  print(max_value) # Output: 50
```

## 2. Fibonacci Sequence

- **How It Works:**
- Create an array fib where fib[i] represents the i-th Fibonacci number.
- Start with fib[0] = 0 and fib[1] = 1.
- Calculate each subsequent Fibonacci number as the sum of the previous two.

- **Example Code:**

```
def fibonacci(n):
  if n <= 1:
  return n
  fib = [0] * (n + 1)
  fib[1] = 1
  for i in range(2, n + 1):
  fib[i] = fib[i - 1] + fib[i - 2]
  return fib[n]
```

191

```
print(fibonacci(5)) # Output: 5
  print(fibonacci(10)) # Output: 55
```

**This approach ensures that students understand the concepts of dynamic programming, the Knapsack Problem, and the Fibonacci Sequence in a fun and engaging way.**

## Recursion

### Introduction to Recursion

**Objective: Explain the concept of recursion and how it works by breaking down a problem into smaller instances of the same problem. Use simple examples and fun analogies to engage young learners.**

### Example: Counting Down with Recursion

- **How It Works:**
- The countdown function takes a number n and prints it.
- If n is greater than 0, it calls itself with n - 1.
- The base case stops the recursion when n is 0.
- **Example Code:**

```
def countdown(n):
  if n <= 0: # Base case
  print("Blast off!")
  else: # Recursive case
  print(n)
  countdown(n - 1)
```

192

countdown(5)

## Example: Factorial with Recursion

- **How It Works:**
- The factorial function takes a number n and returns its factorial.
- If n is 0, it returns 1.
- If n is greater than 0, it returns n multiplied by the factorial of n - 1.
- **Example Code:**

```
def factorial(n):
  if n == 0: # Base case
  return 1
  else: # Recursive case
  return n * factorial(n - 1)
```

```
print(factorial(5)) # Output: 120
```

**This approach ensures that students understand the concept of recursion, including the importance of base and recursive cases, through engaging examples and activities.**

# 23

# Chapter 18 Best Practices and version control

- Writing clean and readable code (PEP 8)

Objective: **Explain the importance of writing clean and readable code using PEP 8 guidelines. Use simple analogies and examples to engage young learners.**

Why Follow PEP 8?

- **Purpose:** To ensure consistency and readability in code.
- **Approach:** Use fun analogies and simple examples to make the guidelines relatable and easy to understand.

## Key PEP 8 Guidelines

1. **Use Meaningful Names:**

- **Explanation:** Choose descriptive names for variables and functions to make the code self-explanatory.
- **Example:**
- Good: "magic_spell"
- Bad: "ms"

1. **Use Spaces Around Operators:**

- **Explanation:** Adding spaces around operators improves readability.
- **Example:**
- Good: "a + b"
- Bad: "a+b"

1. **Indentation:**

- **Explanation:** Proper indentation visually separates blocks of code.
- **Example:**

```
def greet():
    print("Hello!")
```

1. **Keep Lines Short:**

- **Explanation:** Keeping lines under 79 characters ensures

195

they fit within standard display limits.
- **Example:** Ensure each line of code is concise and to the point.

1. **Use Blank Lines to Separate Code:**

- **Explanation:** Blank lines enhance readability by visually separating different sections.
- **Example:**

```
def greet():
  print("Hello!")

def farewell():
  print("Goodbye!")
```

1. **Use Comments to Explain Your Code:**

- **Explanation:** Comments clarify the purpose of code segments for future reference.
- **Example:**

```
# This function greets the user
  def greet():
  print("Hello!")
```

**This approach ensures students grasp the significance of PEP 8 guidelines and apply them effectively to maintain clean and readable code.**

## Code optimization

**Objective: Explain the importance of code optimization and introduce basic strategies to make code run more efficiently. Use simple analogies and examples to engage young learners.**

### Key Optimization Strategies

1. **Use Efficient Data Structures:**

- **Explanation:** Choose appropriate data structures for specific tasks.
- **Example:**
- List for simple collections.
- Dictionary for quick look-ups.

1. **Avoid Unnecessary Calculations:**

- **Explanation:** Store results of calculations to avoid redundant operations.
- **Example:**

```
total = a + b
  print(total)
  print(total)
```

1. **Use Built-in Functions:**

- **Explanation:** Built-in functions are optimized and efficient.

- **Example:**

```
sum(numbers)
```

1. **Avoid Unnecessary Loops:**

- **Explanation:** Minimize nested loops to reduce complexity.
- **Example:**

```
for item in items:
    process(item)
```

1. **Profile Your Code:**

- **Explanation:** Use profiling tools to identify bottlenecks.
- **Example:**

```
import cProfile
cProfile.run('your_function()')
```

**Approach:** Use simple analogies (e.g., toy cars, shortcuts) and practical examples to illustrate each concept, making the learning process engaging and effective for young students.

## Testing (unittest, pytest)

**Objective: Introduce students to the concept of testing, emphasizing its importance in ensuring code reliability. Use simple analogies and examples to make the topic engaging and understandable.**

## Key Testing Concepts

1. **Unit Tests:**

   - **Explanation:** Focus on testing individual functions or methods.
   - **Example:**

```
import unittest

class TestAddFunction(unittest.TestCase):
    def test_add(self):
        self.assertEqual(add(2, 3), 5)
```

1. **Integration Tests:**

   - **Explanation:** Test the interaction between different parts of a program.
   - **Example:**

```
# Assume read_file and process_data are two separate functions
    def test_integration():
    data = read_file('data.txt')
    result = process_data(data)
    assert result == expected_output
```

1. **Using unittest:**

   - **Explanation:** Demonstrate how to set up and run unit tests using the unittest module.

- **Example:**

```
import unittest

class TestAddFunction(unittest.TestCase):
  def test_add(self):
  self.assertEqual(add(2, 3), 5)

if __name__ == '__main__':
  unittest.main()
```

1. **Using pytest:**

- **Explanation:** Simplify the process with pytest, highlighting its ease of use.
- **Example:**

```
def test_add():
  assert add(2, 3) == 5
```

**Approach:** Use relatable analogies (e.g., LEGO building) and practical examples to explain testing concepts. Ensure students understand the importance of testing and how to implement it using unittest and pytest.

# 24

# Version control (Git, GitHub)

**O**bjective: Introduce students to version control using Git and GitHub. Emphasize the importance of tracking changes, collaboration, and safeguarding work. Use simple analogies and practical examples to make the topic engaging and understandable.

Key Concepts:

1. **Version Control:**

- **Explanation:** A system that tracks changes to your code over time.
- **Analogy:** A time machine or photo album for your project.

1. **Git:**

- **Explanation:** A tool to use version control on your computer.
- **Steps to Set Up:**

- Install Git.
- Configure Git with username and email.
- **Fun Tip:** Git is your project's best friend who remembers everything!

1. **GitHub:**

- **Explanation:** A website to store and share your projects.
- **Steps to Use:**
- Create a GitHub account.
- Create a new repository.
- Push your project to GitHub.
- **Fun Tip:** GitHub is a giant library where you can keep your project and share it with friends!

**Approach:** Use relatable analogies (e.g., time machine, photo album) and practical examples to explain version control concepts. Ensure students understand the basic Git commands and how to use GitHub for collaboration and backup.

# 25

# Epilogue

As we conclude this guide, I hope you have found it as rewarding to teach as it was to create. Introducing young minds to programming is not just about imparting knowledge; it's about igniting a passion for learning and discovery. The skills and confidence your students gain from this journey will be invaluable as they navigate their future.

Remember, teaching is not just about delivering content but about creating an environment where curiosity and creativity thrive. Celebrate every small victory and encourage perseverance through challenges.

Thank you for being a part of this incredible journey. Your dedication to nurturing the next generation of coders is truly inspiring. Keep exploring, keep innovating, and most importantly, keep making learning fun!

www.ingramcontent.com/pod-product-compliance
Lightning Source LLC
LaVergne TN
LVHW081525050326
832903LV00025B/1624